Pornography, Indigeneity and Neocolonialism

Pornography, Indigeneity and Neocolonialism examines how pornography operates as a representational system that authenticates settler colonies, focusing on American and Australian examples to reveal how pornography encodes whiteness, pleasure, colonisation and Indigeneity.

This is the first text to use decolonial and queer theory to examine the role of pornography in America and Australia, as part of a network of neocolonial strategies that "naturalise" occupation. It is also the first study to focus on Indigenous people in pornography, providing a framework for understanding explicit representations of First Nations peoples. *Pornography, Indigeneity and Neocolonialism* defines the characteristics of heterosexual pornography in settler colonies, exposing how the landscape is presented as both exotic and domestic – a land of taboo pleasures that is tamed and occupied by and through white bodies. Examining the absence of Indigenous porn actors and arguing against the hypervisual fetishising of Black bodies that dominates racialised porn discourse, the book places this absence within the context of legal, political and military neocolonial Indigenous elimination strategies.

This book will be of key interest to researchers and students studying porn studies, media and film studies, critical race studies and whiteness studies.

Tim Gregory is a Lecturer in Art at UNSW, Sydney. He is an artist and writer who researches the intersection of pornography, colonialism, art and politics. He is interested in experimental art and writing that critiques heterosexual culture. Tim has exhibited work at the Museum of Contemporary Art (Sydney), the Art Gallery of NSW and the Venice Arsenale. He has been selected for the Arte Laguna Prize, 8th Biennial of Contemporary Textile Art and The Blake Prize. He has published in *Porn Studies*, *Sexualities*, *CSR* and the *Space and Culture Journal*.

Focus on Global Gender and Sexuality

Trans Dilemmas
Stephen Kerry

Gender, Sport and the Role of the Alter Ego in Roller Derby
Colleen E. Arendt

The Poetry of Arab Women from the Pre-Islamic Age to Andalusia
Wessam Elmeligi

Interviews with Mexican Women
We Don't Talk About Feminism Here
Carlos M. Coria-Sanchez

Pornography, Indigeneity and Neocolonialism
Tim Gregory

www.routledge.com/Focus-on-Global-Gender-and-Sexuality/book-series/FGGS

Pornography, Indigeneity and Neocolonialism

Tim Gregory

LONDON AND NEW YORK

First published 2020 by Routledge

2 Park Square, Milton Park, Abingdon, Oxon OX14 4RN

605 Third Avenue, New York, NY 10017

Routledge is an imprint of the Taylor & Francis Group, an informa business

First issued in paperback 2021

Copyright © 2020 Tim Gregory

The right of Tim Gregory to be identified as author of this work has been asserted by him in accordance with sections 77 and 78 of the Copyright, Designs and Patents Act 1988.

All rights reserved. No part of this book may be reprinted or reproduced or utilised in any form or by any electronic, mechanical, or other means, now known or hereafter invented, including photocopying and recording, or in any information storage or retrieval system, without permission in writing from the publishers.

Notice:

Product or corporate names may be trademarks or registered trademarks, and are used only for identification and explanation without intent to infringe.

Publisher's Note

The publisher has gone to great lengths to ensure the quality of this reprint but points out that some imperfections in the original copies may be apparent.

British Library Cataloguing-in-Publication Data
A catalogue record for this book is available from the British Library

Library of Congress Cataloging-in-Publication Data
Names: Gregory, Tim (Lecturer in art), author.
Title: Pornography, indigeneity and neocolonialism / Tim Gregory.
Description: Abingdon, Oxon ; New York, NY : Routledge, 2020. | Series: Focus on global gender and sexuality | Includes bibliographical references and index. Identifiers: LCCN 2019055707 (print) | LCCN 2019055708 (ebook) | ISBN 9780367193300 (hbk) | ISBN 9780429201776 (ebk) | ISBN 9780429510441 (Adobe PDF) | ISBN 9780429513879 (epub) | ISBN 9780429517303 (mobi)
Subjects: LCSH: Pornography. | Indigenous peoples. | Sex.
Classification: LCC HQ471 .G737 2020 (print) | LCC HQ471 (ebook) | DDC 306/.77/1–dc23
LC record available at https://lccn.loc.gov/2019055707
LC ebook record available at https://lccn.loc.gov/2019055708

ISBN: 978-0-367-19330-0 (hbk)
ISBN: 978-1-03-217372-6 (pbk)
DOI: 10.4324/9780429201776

Typeset in Sabon
by Wearset Ltd, Boldon, Tyne and Wear

For Sacha and Laura

Contents

	Acknowledgements	viii
	Introduction	1
1	Colonial pornographic exotica	24
2	The absence of Indigenous people in pornography	53
3	The colonial cumshot	78
	Bibliography	103
	Index	113

Acknowledgements

I acknowledge the Bidjigal and Gadigal peoples of the Eora nation as the traditional custodians of the land on which I live and work. I pay my respects to Elders past and present and extend this respect to all Aboriginal and Torres Strait Islander people. Sovereignty was never ceded. I also want to acknowledge that acknowledgement is not enough.

An earlier version of Chapter 1 was published as *The maintenance of white heteronormativity in porn films that use Australia as an exotic location* in Porn Studies, vol. 4, no. 1, pp. 88–104 (access www.tandfonline.com/). It has been revised and updated for publication here, with permission from the original publisher.

I want to specifically thank my loyal dog pack, pup (Astrid), new dog (Brooks), old dog (Dave) and big dog (Uros). They have provided me with the support I needed to realise this project. This text is very much a pack effort.

Finally, I wish to acknowledge the students and tutors in the courses I teach at UNSW Art & Design, especially *Pornography, Art and Politics* and *Post-Pornographic Bodies*. Many of the ideas in this text have emerged from these students and tutors' dedication to radical politics.

Introduction

Pornography is the most invisible yet abundant representational mode. Until the 1990s it was largely ignored as a system worthy of investigation by academics, sociologists and cultural producers. While popular cultural forms like television, radio, advertising and film have long been assessed for their impact on forming personal, communal and national identity, until recently explicit displays of sex have escaped such attention. Pornography has not only evaded critical investigation, but it is characterised by its illusiveness and exceptionality; that is, it is considered more indexical than other genres and hence primarily affective rather than symbolic or textural. The viewer singularly masturbates to pornography, they do not read, synthesise, refer, recognise, share, relate or contextualise the imagery. This means that pornography is not seen alongside or within other genres of representation. The exceptional status of pornography means it appears immune to strategies applied to other representational systems. Porn is not considered to have a message or a productive utility, and porn is not deployed nor calculated for political or social gain. It simply designates sexual preference, or more often perversion. Its economics is one of exploitation rather than accumulation. While the art historian Kenneth Clark (1972) connected pornography to propaganda, he did so in order to dismiss it as the lowest form of imagery, rather than to suggest that pornography is deliberately used to manipulate public opinion. However, this definition of porn is a product of porn's own mythmaking, perpetuated by the fear and desire that the mere mention of it inspires. This myth disguises porn's larger operation and integration across representational systems that structure nationalism and maintain settler states.

Linda Williams (2014, p. 37) defines pornography as 'two contradictory things at once: documents of sexual acts, and fantasies spun around knowing the pleasure or pain of those acts. Pornography studies needs to remember that it must always exist at the problematic site of this limit'. This book asks what happens if we think of pornography outside of this limit? What if the contradiction is not found in the content of pornography but in the manner of its distribution? What if it is not a document of sex? And what if the fantasies that are spun are not directly related to the acts depicted? If we can expand pornography beyond this site, can we recognise a different, more integrated fantasy that is directly connected to the formation and affirmation of settler sexuality.

My aim is to demonstrate how contemporary pornography is structured by colonial contact with Indigenous sex and sexuality. I argue that pornography affirms colonisation by naturalising settler sexuality across patriarchal image networks. Pornography is a representational system that developed from frontier, colonial sexual violence that enforced a binary between Native and non-Native sex. This binary, as Morgensen (2011) argues, is the foundational queering that establishes modern sexuality, placing the processes of colonisation and the exclusion of Indigenous people as central to contemporary discourses on sex and desire. Pornography's duty was, and remains, to make settler and Indigenous futurity incompatible through explicit displays of sex. Specifically, I will demonstrate how porn's racialisations are built on an originary judgement of Native/non-Native which denies pornographic representation to Indigenous people. This censorship not only prevents access for Indigenous people to identify with, contest and contribute to their sexual representation, but prevents settler fantasies of "Natives" from being discussed, desired and critiqued. Pornography accrues colonial value through imaging racial and sexual hierarchies which fluctuate depending on the ideological demands of settlement. However, all bodies imaged in pornography have some value and position in settler sexuality. The absence of Indigenous people from pornography's racialisations deliberately places Indigenous sex and futures outside colonial value. The silence in porn and in porn studies around Indigenous representation is what this book attempts to address. In particular, it suggests that this invisibility in porn, that has remained consistent since the early twentieth century, is not a peripheral concern, but an active repression operating at the centre of pornography's monopoly on imaging modern sexuality and desire. Because of this, pornography can be analysed to reveal histories of colonial violence perpetuated through narratives of incompatibility and elimination. Crucially I do not suggest this is found in certain types of pornography, but that pornography itself is a technology of colonialism. The absence of Indigenous people is not resolved by calls for inclusion, because inclusion in pornography can only further pre-destined colonial positions. Pornography is a symptom *and* cause of settler sexuality, and only a total transformation of representational frameworks could begin to account for explicit Indigenous sexual futures and desires.

Terminology

When I use the term "porn" I am referring to heteronormative porn, or heteroporn. It is important to note that there are many pornographies, and not all are encompassed by the term porn. For the purpose of this book I will be using the terms porn/heteroporn, post-pornography and queer porn to demarcate these differences. I define queer porn as porn that resists normative modes, models and/or distribution. It is structurally and narratively opposed to heteroporn, although not always directly reactive or referential. Queer porn has its own histories and archives that run alongside the history of heteroporn. Post-pornography is a term that emerges from specific queer activists and artists in America, Spain and Germany (Gregory and Lorange 2018). In theory and art, post-porn refers to the denaturalising of sex and the decentring of the spectator. This book follows in that tradition, however because of my focus on the distribution of contemporary porn, I define post-pornography differently to refer to the expanded representative network of contemporary porn. This definition of post-pornography locates it in the increased availability and integration of pornography into sex largely as a result of the internet. The ease of access to consume and produce pornography, particularly for white men, has rapidly expanded its representational power producing networks of image sharing and consuming that have developed cultural logics, syntaxes and hierarchies. In relation to questions of technology, access and volume, post-porn can be heteronormative or queer. There is a distinction between post-porn heterosex and post-porn queer sex, however both involve the blurring of the boundary between image and body, technology and sex. In a post-porn context sexual gestures which might typically be defined as straight or queer become more fluid. Instead of locating the differences in specific content, a more useful distinction can be made by following Ahmed (2006) and Paasonen's (2011) call for the critical and analytical curiosity of the porn producer and viewer. An analytic curiosity has yet to be turned towards questions of Indigenous representation and participation in pornography. It is through this distinction that I situate my critique of settlers as un-analytic, post-porn spectators and producers.

One of the issues that porn scholarship confronts is its tendency to order its study around the spectacular and enticing categories the porn industry uses. As Williams (2014) notes porn studies has a problematic and close relationship to the porn industry and focusing on the sex acts depicted and their seemingly obvious orientation and meaning can miss the larger, more subtle operations that have integrated porn into hierarchical non-pornographic representational structures. More broadly the problem that the discussion (be it academic, social or educational) of pornography often falls into is a focus on the content rather than the context (McNair 2014; Paasonen *et al.* 2007). This tends to privilege the explicit over the absent, as well as isolating the discussion to the assumed boundaries of the pornographic – the documentation of sex, and fantasies directly connected to the documentation. However, centring analytic curiosity on the *context* of pornography reveals its enmeshed operative power across publicly non-pornographic heteropatriarchal institutions and image distribution networks. I will start by situating the discussion of pornography around a series of contradictory characteristics – namely how it is invisible *and* known, spectacular *and* mundane, domestic *and* distributed. These are the properties that inform the context that pornography both shapes and is shaped by. Unpacking the operations of heteroporn is an important step in understanding how such texts function within and towards ideologies and contexts – and specifically for this book, how these operations are integral to the justification and maintenance of white futurity in settler colonies.

Invisible *and* known

As access to porn increased in the mid nineteenth and early twentieth century due to mechanical reproduction so did the moral outrage – porn spread beyond the secret collections of the wealthy bourgeois and was available to the middle and working classes.[1] The assumed ability for pornography to corrupt and deprave only became a concern with its larger distribution. The fear of porn for the masses was a fear of it inciting a bacchanalian revolution in which people (predominantly men), unable to tell representation from reality, would refuse heteronormative structures (marriage, home ownership, wage labour) as the only outlet for sexual desires. As Donzelot (1979) notes, the rise of the "family" in the nineteenth century is directly tied to the disciplining of the body under capitalism. The danger of pornography was that it imaged a world of sexual pleasure that existed outside the family. More importantly, such images could be surreptitiously brought into the family home in the guise of fitness magazines and innocuously titled periodicals. Access to pornography could threaten the emerging repressive and puritan "iron cage" of the frugal middle class (Weber 2003). Pornography had found its way into the iron cage bringing with it a potential to corrupt the base unit of capitalism – the normative family. The perfect image of this fear is captured in a photograph taken in a *Home Depo*. It shows a smart fridge, which features a screen connected to the internet, and on the screen the home page of *Pornhub*. The "smart" fridge, a symbol of domestic efficiency or the cold heart of the nuclear family, is revealed to be just another node for the distribution of porn.[2] Because of this prevailing fear, the definition of pornography changes in the twentieth century to be directly related to its medium and means of distribution rather than its content.

The invention of photography signals the modern era of porn, and as Solomon-Godeau (1986, p. 87) states, 'it seems reasonable to assume that almost as soon as there were viable daguerreotypes, there were pornographic ones'. By 1874, 130,000 pornographic photographs had been seized by the London police and the distinction between "dangerous" pornographic images and "erotic" texts begins to emerge. By 1986, the US Attorney General's Commission on Pornography (1986, p. 1709) argued '[text requires] more real thought and less almost reflexive reaction than does the more typical pornographic item'. The class bias here is obvious, pornographic images were thought to have more affinity with the masses, who would not, or could not, *read* the image. While photography has been deployed for spectacular effect in advertising and propaganda, photographic pornography remains largely invisible. Censorship of pornography has been favoured over using it to evoke a mass of sentiments in the public service of the state or capitalism (although there are notable exceptions). Instead, pornography was deployed through invisible patriarchal networks in an attempt to keep its feared antinormative message isolated to individuals who were thought capable of *reading* the image (i.e. integrating it into normativity) rather than reacting to its indexical power and demanding the right to public, identified antinormative sex.

Censoring pornography by restricting access to distribution networks is not only class and gender based, it is also racialised. Like the working class, non-white bodies are assumed to be more easily corrupted by pornography. The *Little Children are Sacred* report, commissioned by the Northern Territory Government in Australia and used as justification for the suspension of the Racial Discrimination Act and the declaration of a state of emergency in the Northern Territory, states that pornography 'encourages [Aboriginal men] to act out the fantasies they've seen in magazines' (Wild and Anderson 2007, p. 200). Porn is seen as erasing the distinction between representation and reality, both in that the fucking it depicts is "real", and that the viewer is compelled to make the image "real". Disguised as a medium specific argument about the nature of photography and video, it is in fact a racist determination about the capacity to separate image from act. At first glance there is a double subjugation occurring here, in that those typically denied access to pornography are also those most likely to be represented in pornography. Certain bodies are deemed to be more indexical than others. Photography of naked white men are held within histories of science, sport and medicine and are less indexical than images of women or people of colour (Davis 1991). Within these histories naked white men represent the normative standard and come to act as symbols for these disciplines. In contrast, Black and brown bodies exist in these disciplines to be scrutinised as non-consenting objects of study.[3] The white naked male is the control in such scientific experiments, and hence valued for its assumed consistency and invisibility. In pornography the more indexical a certain body is declared the more value they have, and conversely the more they are "protected" from the harm that is assumed to come from this increased indexicality (Chun and Friedland 2015). This is the dialectic of pornographic distribution, whereby any increase in representation is simultaneously the removal of agency and access to the person represented.[4] However, Indigenous people sit outside of this violence of double subjugation, and as this book will show, they are denied representation, agency and access.

Pornography's inability to be framed outside of content, while in practice being defined by context is the reason for the endurance of Justice Potter Stewart's (1964) 'I know it if I see it' definition of pornography. This definition allows for pornography to be uncritically flexible, as any change cannot be recognised if pornography is always simply "known". At the same time, it is a rigid definition, as what is "known" (marked by arousal or disgust) can only be porn. However, it is worth being precise here, for what Potter is appealing to is the idea that one does not need to have seen pornography to know it; that it is a universally recognisable representational form – that it transcends the coding of its representation. But what is actually being said here is that he (and the hetero-male public) has seen a lot of porn, and hence they know it when they see it, but cannot admit to this knowledge as it would transgress social norms. The heavily codified language of pornography that is taught through formal and informal patriarchal systems is publicly declared "natural". It assumes we know what sex is, and what it should look like. For the hetero-public the combined explicitness of the medium (film and photography) and content (fucking) means that pornography cannot be misinterpreted, or perhaps more importantly, interpreted. This naturalisation has implications beyond public denial, it means that the taxonomies of pornography, which I will show are products of settler sexuality, are taken to be ahistorical.

The paradox of pornography is that it survives through a claim to exceptionality that protects its producers and consumers but profits from its total integration and familiarity. The phantasma of pornography is not the narrative of pool boys and delivery men, it is the phantasma of a public performance of invisibility. Porn operates as a *system of representation* by denying its systemic qualities. Part of this denial is because of its characterisation as a disturbance to identity (Nead 2002; Bataille 1962; Sontag 1982) and as having a carnal resonance (Passonen 2011). Porn has these qualities, but porn's power is drawn from this affective potential being regulated by visual codes and maintained from within a tightly structured and integrated representational system that is performatively invisible. The question that Paul B. Preciado (2015) asks of pornography is 'how to displace the visual codes that historically have served to designate the normal or the abject?' This is largely the work of porn studies, however, part of this question is also the need to demonstrate that pornography *is* a system of visual codes. What if we thought about porn outside of sex? What if porn had very little to do with sex? What if porn, as an independent, yet connected representational system of visual codes forms and maintains identity (even while threatening to undo it)? Sexual identity is part of this, but no less important is its projection and protection of the boundaries of race, class, gender, nationalism, age, fashion, interior design and so on. This book suggests that porn speaks to race beyond the intersection of sex and race. In writing about the nature of a settler colony, Wolfe (1999, p. 214) argues that 'what needs to be written in is not the agency of the colonised but the total context of inscription'. Pornography is part of the total context of inscription in a settler colony. The inscription is not undone by displacing visual codes or "allowing" the pornographic agency of the colonised from within a settler colony. Instead I aim to show how pornography inscribes race, invasion, dispossession, property, assimilation and Indigeneity in settler colonies.

Pornographic spectacle

In explicitly displaying fucking bodies, porn is spectacular by default. Its spectacularity is seemingly the dominant reason for its easy identification and exceptionality. However, I want to suggest that porn is not a spectacle in itself, but rather is spectacular at the moment it becomes public. It is in the mundanity of pornography – as a domestic consumerable – that its true power to be integrated into heteronormativity lies. The history of modern and contemporary pornography is punctuated by moments of high visibility, which treat pornography as an acute issue requiring legislation, condemnation and censorship. Prurient public forums that examine the damaging effects of pornography (such as the Meese Commission and the Backpage legislation in America, and the Porn Report in Australia) emerge in response to the growing visibility of groups whose sexuality is feared – the Meese Commission policed gay and lesbian sex, the Backpage legislation targeted sex workers, and the Porn Report focused on the containment of adolescent sex. The political violence of these moments is that they connect the hypocritical universal public distain of pornography directly to non-normative sex.

The activation of pornography as a spectacular political tool can be understood through Jacques Rancière's (2004) notion of the distribution of the sensible, which addresses how images are distributed into public understanding. The distribution of the sensible is most active at the threshold of the visible and is the normative force that either censors and represses the invisible or incorrectly distributes the invisible into extant normative representational hierarchies. For Rancière, the specific power of aesthetics produces a dynamic, political function that delimits and structures the seeable, sayable and doable. Rancière's definition is useful for discussing porn because it takes into account the affective, somatic register of images that interacts with and formulates experience. As he states,

> appearance is not an illusion that is opposed to the real. It is the introduction of a visible into the field of experience, which then modifies the regime of the visible. It is not opposed to reality. It splits reality and reconfigures it as double.
>
> (Rancière 1999, p. 99)

For Bennett (2012, p. 2) this conception of the distribution of visible 'reconfigures the aesthetic as the site for the systematic ordering of sense experience – a kind of regime of the sensible, which in turn establishes the political function of aesthetics'. Pornography seems to sit well with Rancière's aesthetics of sense experience, as porn is often feared for having affective or bodily control over its viewers. This emphasis is also because pornography has been used as a marker of anti-art and anti-aesthetics, its stubborn persistence is argued to be a result of affective, biological and psychological power rather than aesthetic power. As Nead (2002, p. 28) describes,

> the pure aesthetic experience is posed as a consolidation of individual subjectivity, it can be seen in terms of the framing of the subject. In contrast, the experience of pornography is described as a kind of disturbance, it presents the possibility of an undoing of identity.

Rancière offers a way to understand pornography as both disruptive and structural, affective and political. Porn is not an either/or but rather is always both.

This operation is perhaps most obvious when queer sex is registered as public. The distribution of the sensible typically starts with public outrage as a pretext to regulate private, personal and identitarian spaces. Publicly funded investigations into pornography are often about preventing representations of queer sex being distributed into heteroporn – although in reality it is about slowing down the distribution so that it can be misappropriated and capitalised on by heteropatriarchy. Heteroporn has a different integration into the visible, for while queer sex has to fight for identity, heteroporn fights for invisibility. This produces a contradiction as to how it is distributed into the sensible, whereby it is successfully integrated into the sensible – into the known – but remains invisible. As Paasonen (2011, p. 2) argues heteroporn paradoxically occupies the 'ambivalent position as a public secret – ubiquitous yet effaced and silenced'. Because of this, pornography is by default "normative" but can be activated publicly, and spectacularly, to signify perversion. This is why queer sex – as something that is visible, confronting, deconstructive and confusing to the sensible – can be attacked at any moment by connecting it to the distribution of pornography. Queer sex is assumed to be more explicit, more "sex" obsessed, in part, because of this forced connection. Queer sex becomes read through pornography and hence the same extensive invisible distribution network that protects heteroporn spreads panic that queer sex is suddenly infiltrating everywhere and nowhere, turning it into a question of heteronormativity (protecting children, wives, private property, reputations and so on). Pornography operates normatively when invisible, and as a signifier of perversion when visible. In this way, pornography operates uniquely in the distribution of the sensible.

The problem of anti-spectacular porn

Pornography – understood as the public visibility of fucking bodies – is spectacular and because of this porn is commonly used as a metaphor and an adjective to denote spectacularity. Frederic Jameson (2013) goes as far as to label everything visual as essentially pornographic. He critiques the contemporary spectacle as having to end in mindless rapt fascination and reflexively connects this directly to pornography. The pornographic stands in for the postmodern condition, where images have replaced or at least been inserted between bodies. Following Debord's (2014, p. 21) definition of the spectacle as 'a relation between people that is mediated by images', Jameson uses pornography as both the exemplar of the society of the spectacle and as an adjective to describe all mass media. The reproduction of images (rather than bodies) is the goal of porn, and the success of porn suggests a larger postmodern victory where even our most basic instincts have been incorporated by the image – we prefer to masturbate than procreate. Porn's success in co-opting bodies for the reproduction of the image is central to critiques of spectacular culture.

When porn is used as an adjective it denotes a type of uncritical, consumerist hyperreality. Food porn, war porn, torture porn takes something visceral, quintessentially of the body, and turns it into images that forgo the body (at least the body of those consuming the images). The absurdity of food produced for the image (turmeric lattes that are the filter spice of Instagram), war created for the image ("Shock and Awe" in Iraq) and torture created for the image (Abu Ghraib torture and the subsequent meme, "doing a Lynndie"[5]) invert the "logic" of these acts, which are founded on the original pornographic inversion of the orgasm created for the camera. Porn is recognised as either a perversion of morality or representation and despite proponents of each being diametrically opposed, they draw the same conclusion, which is that porn is the making of something that was authentic, inauthentic. In order to be spectacular, porn must be explicit, but in doing so, as Baudrillard (2003, p. 23) writes, it is 'without genuine pleasure'. One's position on porn becomes a

Introduction 11

shorthand signifier for complex theoretical and political positions: for postmodernists porn marks the victory of the image over the act, for conservatives porn demonstrates the perversion of sex outside marriage, and for feminists porn is proof that male pleasure is predicated on the subjugation and humiliation of another's body. I do not want to step through the alternate histories of porn that do not align with these positions as the discipline of porn studies emerges from other histories in feminism, film studies and critical theory that contests these generalisations. I want to focus on the anti-spectacular content, operation and distribution of pornography as a deliberate strategy to disguise the extent of its authenticating power across colonial heteropatriarchy.

The vast majority of porn is not spectacular. Most porn is, in fact, mundane, ordinary, boring. The porn that is consumed (rather than made public) is anti-spectacular. The difference between porn and food porn, for example, is that food porn seeks a public audience through the aesthetic tropes of pornography. Like Justice Potter Stewart, food porn says we know you've seen porn, but here is an image that can be openly shared and celebrated – it is spectacular because it is not-porn porn. The porn that necessitates private browsing is quotidian porn, it is characterised by distracted, disinterested, non-linear viewing. Experiencing porn is a relational activity across different and often completely disconnected fragments of media. It is also relational to specific spaces and times – anti-spectacular porn is related to domestic space, to domestic internet providers, and to leisure time that affords privacy. As such, watching porn is not singular but is a necessarily relational activity with a set of privileges that permits or denies its viewing. It intersects with many public points (ISPs, VPNs, internet browsers, terms and conditions, nondescript business names, teleconferencing and messaging apps) from whom pseudo-anonymity is purchased. The crucial point is that porn cannot be accurately accounted for independently of these relations.

The problem of discussing anti-spectacular porn is similar to the problem of analysing a very different representational genre – family photographs. Batchen (2008) points out, family photos are one of the largest genres of photography, but once removed from their relationship to the domestic they become something entirely different. Visual analysis of family photographs selects "random" anti-spectacular examples because iconic family photos are anathema. However, such analysis struggles beyond a simplistic taxonomy, because it cannot account for what each family photograph *does*. As Rose (2016, p. 137) argues these chosen family photographs are 'displaced into the public realm and thereby changed into something other than itself'. Porn shares many similarities with family photographs – it is organised in simple taxonomies, struggles to be described beyond specific utility and is ubiquitous yet largely invisible (social media has changed this for family photos, but its net of relations remain still closed to those who know the subjects independently from the image). Porn and family photographs enter public discourse in the same way, they become exceptional and spectacular simply because they have become public. The vast majority of porn and family photographs cannot structurally be discussed in public, because making it visible violates its specific and necessarily invisible operation in heteronormativity. Porn is not only structurally similar to family photographs, it occupies the same space physically and conceptually (for example, the *Porn Hub* smart fridge occupies the same gallery space as family photographs held up by novelty magnets). Heteroporn and family photographs both maintain the domestic fantasy of the happy family and the desiring married couple. In a post-porn context this connection collapses even further, with the cameras used to take family photographs the same ones that are used to take pornographic images and videos. The production of pornography has become part of heterosex, as both a document and an incentive. Although taboos clearly differentiate these genres, technologies converge such that cameras, SD cards and hard drives share pornographic and family image archives.

The problem with analysing domestic pornography is also identified in art history. Kenneth Clark describes the pornographic frescos found in homes in Pompeii that date back to the Roman empire as 'documentaries [that] have nothing to do with art' (quoted in Longford 1972, p. 100).[6] This assumes they have no public duty and that the domestic realm is devoid of aesthetics while also connecting the pornographic to truth telling by referring to them as documentaries. Clark makes this argument for the Lord Longford's report into pornography in 1972, as such it is not an historical account, but an attempt to give historical weight to a contemporary definition of pornography. In doing so Clark, and the report, dismisses domestic pornographic imagery as noise, which, as Rancière *et al.* (2001) argues is how domestic speech is made publicly unintelligible. The deliberate separation of "domestic" and "representation" works to disguise or prevent the politics of the domestic from being recognised. For representations by women and people of colour, a forced "domestic" distribution deliberately attempts to prevent a shared politics from forming within and across oppressed groups and breaching public discourse. However, for pornographic representation, whose primary domestic audience also dominates public discourse, its "domestication" eases its invisible distribution across larger representational systems. The unique distribution of porn means that its public invisibility and domestic consumption is the very thing that makes it intelligible to patriarchal networks that chooses who, when and how to spectacularise its sporadic public appearance.

Porn studies encounters the same problem of necessarily making porn public, unintentionally spectacularising porn *so it can be studied*. The consequence of this is that any discussion of pornography, including academic discussion, becomes spectacular and makes it difficult to access the mundane workings of heteroporn without that access itself being labelled a-typical. My own publications on porn reveal this, as they receive abnormally high metrics for public engagement. This is because of the mostly critical reaction that the titles and keywords of my articles garner on social media. Strangely this also makes my scholarship more visible within my institution, demonstrating the structural bind all porn scholars, activists and queer pornographers face in attempting to reveal a system that demands it be made public on its own spectacular terms. By focusing on the structures and distribution of heteroporn across settler colonies I hope to position the inevitable spectacularising of my discussion as a specific manifestation of porn's everyday, distributed, domestic use.[7]

Settler colonies

This book examines the connection between pornography and settler colonies, however the definition of a settler colony is not singular. The history and impact of settler colonies is different in each instance, ranging from countries where the settlers declared independence (America) to Federations with legislative independence (Australia, New Zealand, Canada), to countries more commonly associated with postcolonial studies where independence was fought for and won by the Indigenous populations (South Africa, India, Indonesia). These three categories have created a hierarchy between Indigenous and settler independence status that replicates East/West, Black/white, first/third world, developed/developing bias. The ambiguity in defining settler colonisation is a result of the term's relatively short academic history, with it only becoming a separate field of critical scholarship in the 1990s (Veracini 2013). Settlement's relationship to colonisation was originally obscured through the denial of Indigenous occupation and sovereignty, with the settler's connection seen to be only between the "virgin" land and the metropole. As Lorenzo Veracini (2013, p. 135) states this "pioneering" logic established 'long-lasting traits of settler colonial political traditions: a gendered order, a focus on mononuclear familial relations and reproduction, and the production of assets transferable across generations'.

The first wave of decolonialism after the Second World War was focused on areas where the settler populations were in the minority. As Shepard (2006) argues, decolonial and postcolonial studies developed from this wave of independence, and in particular out of the context of Algeria. Indigenous people in ongoing settler colonies were largely left out of this discourse (Mignolo 2011). This history tends to focus on decolonisation as a process that starts in the mid twentieth century (and around key symbolic points such as the 1993 *Draft Declaration on the Rights of Indigenous Peoples*, ratified in 2007), rather than recognising the long histories of Indigenous resistance and decolonial acts that predate internationally recognised movements (Mar 2016; Moreton-Robinson 2015). Additionally, the centring of nationhood and international Indigenous rights and legal discourses has been critiqued as restricting decolonial futures to the histories and legacies of this first wave of decolonialisation (Coulthard 2018).

Alongside this history, the economic success of ongoing settler colonies following the Second World War resulted in the classification of "second world" (Slemon 1990) to differentiate settler states from metropoles and the "third world". Settler colonies that maintained a profitable exploitative economy based on white nationalist cultures and politics were described as the 'most advanced stage of white colonial expansion' (Ferro 1997, p. 211). While such settler colonies could not be the "first world" because of their lack of pedigree, they could be 'ultra-colonial' (Anderson 1961) and aimed to demonstrate the excessive production possible within settler structures. These states were racially and economically separated from the "third world" which were predominantly postcolonial states where Indigenous populations achieved national independence (Denoon 1979). Following this, Manuel and Posluns (2018) establish the term "fourth world" to describe Indigenous people who are outside the second and third world. Kelley (2017) notes that in the 1970s settler colonies typically referred to Southern African states where the white colonisers required both the land and the labour of Native populations. As such the distinction between exploitation colonies and settler colonies has not historically been determined by the status of Native labour. It is only in the 1980s, with the rise of Indigenous land rights cases that Australia, America, New Zealand and Canada start to become conceptualised as ongoing settler colonies rather than as "young" nations.

The need for settler colonial studies as an autonomous field emerges out of this context, and positions Indigenous histories, experience and cultures as existing before colonisation and continuing across, against and within colonial structures. In this sense, settler colonisation is both an invasion and a structure that is defined by colonial contact with Indigenous people (Byrd 2011). Contemporary settler colonial scholarship examines the perspective of the colonised to analyse countries whose Indigenous populations have historically and contemporarily used and subverted colonial networks for the underground transmission of anti-colonial messages, resistance and solidarity. Tracey Banivanua Mar's (2016, p. 10) excellent history of these invisible networks across the Asia Pacific demonstrates how we might consider these Indigenous populations as separate but linked by 'subaltern, subjugated and subversive webs of connections'. It is important to note, as Paisley (2003) observes, that the contemporary understanding of settler colonialism is largely developed in Australian scholarship which aims to show the relationship between processes of settlement and colonisation. As Veracini (2013, p. 314) argues, in settler colonial studies 'colonialism and settler colonialism should be understood in their dialectical relation: neither entirely separate nor part of the same conceptual field'. This means that we can understand settler colonisation as having specificity *and* as implicated in transnational colonial structures.[8]

This book refers to American and Australian examples, politics and contexts, but does not aim to universalise these examples to all Indigenous people in these settler states, or those outside of them. However, it does understand that both the coloniser and the colonised use transnational networks that means the Native American and Aboriginal focus of this book has significance that radiates outwards and inwards beyond its specificity. The intersection of decolonial theory with queer theory and porn studies provides a framework to critique the post-pornographic transcultural settler.

Sex in settler colonies

Patrick Wolfe (1999, p. 204) makes a distinction between settler colonies and exploitation colonies based on what he terms an "elimination logic". He states,

> Analytically ... it can be seen how the logic of elimination, most crudely manifest in the initial massacres, has persisted into the present by way of a number of strategic transformations. This continuity proceeds from Australian society's primary determination as a settler-colonial state, founded on what I have termed a negative articulation. So far as the present is concerned, over the key question of land, Australian policy continues to be exclusive rather than inclusive in that, at the price of a minimal enfranchisement, the bulk of the Indigenous population is eliminated from the reckoning.

He describes a 'repressive authenticity' that 'detaches Aboriginality from the body' (Wolfe 1999, p. 184), meaning that the process of settlement – sexual violence, miscegenation and murder – erase Indigeneity until finally no one can claim to be Indigenous. Similarly Tuck and Yang (2012, p. 12) argue that 'Native Americanness is subtractive: Native Americans are constructed to become fewer in number and less Native, but never exactly white, over time'. Underpinning repressive authenticity is an economic imperative. As Wolfe (1999, p. 2) states 'in the settler-colonial economy, it is not the colonist but the native who is superfluous'. Veracini (2013) and Kelley (2017) argue that such a characterisation does not adequately describe all settler colonies, nor reflect the histories of Native labour in colonies. However, the elimination logic as a cultural and ideological settler structure is useful in framing the critique of settler sexuality and pornography.

Ann Laura Stoler's (2010) critical decentring of heterosexuality from enlightenment and European origins is crucial to understanding how pornography is structured by settler sexuality. It is not that colonial desires appropriate, exaggerate and attach themselves to pornography's pre-existing gendered and racial hierarchies, but that pornography is an explicit technology of colonialism. Morgensen (2011) argues the first queering was of Indigenous sexualities, which in turn led to the invention of heterosexuality. As Moten (2015) writes 'the ante normative comes first. The ante-normative is "e" which means it comes first, the normative is the after affect, it's a response to the irregular'. Settlers confronted Indigenous futurities that had to be erased, hence settler sexuality was defined against these futures. As such settler sexuality was formed in the colonies as a white supremacist, anti-Native, bio-reproductive coupling that was exported back to the metropoles and eventually became heterosexuality.

Recognising settler sexuality not as a mutation of heterosexuality, but its foundation, is crucial in understanding how race is central to heteronormativity and its representation in pornography. Further how the existing racialised structure of pornography is built on a Native/non-Native determination that operates at the centre of pornography. This binary is the primary judgement that determines what bodies (non-Native) are allowed racially eroticised representative value and what bodies (Native) are refused sexualised representation. The use of the term "Native" in pornography as a micro, remainder category for non-white bodies that are not "Black" (African American) or otherwise racialised is a symptom of this originary judgement. The confused use of "Native" in heteroporn indicates its inability to conceive of Blackness outside of fetishistic slave narratives embedded in North American histories of exploitation. Recognising the development of modern and contemporary pornography as a coproduct of settler sexuality positions heteroporn as ideologically designed to support colonial futurity and racially locate value and position within settler hierarchies. Settler sexuality's "naturalisation" through heterosexuality produces deliberate slippages between white supremacism, heterosex and colonisation that are witnessed in heteroporn. Pornography as the representational arm of settler sexuality reveals these connections through its categorisation, distribution, privileging and exclusion.

The exclusion of Indigenous people in pornography has violent impacts on Indigenous people by refusing sexual representation and enforcing an elimination logic. It also structures settlers use of heteroporn, preventing settlers' sexual fantasies of Indigenous people from being represented. This means that while complex, counter and radical readings of racialised porn, such as those by Jennifer Nash (2014), offer critical pathways through Blackness in pornography, no such potential exists for Indigenous representation. This is especially concerning as these pathways were largely developed from within settler states. A broader examination of heteroporn is required to develop a framework for critiquing how it is integrated into settlement narratives and violence that deny Indigenous existence. This has global relevance, particularly for white people and settlers as my/their ease of access to pornography and my/their implication in colonisation is universal. I have this privilege of agency and access, and I acknowledge that those silenced by the structures I articulate remain silenced. I also recognise the danger that my approach "domesticates decolonization" (Tuck and Yang 2012) and attempts to convert my/settler guilt into ongoing occupation (Mawhinney 1999; Radcliffe 2017), especially as I use Mar's more open definition of decolonisation. However I am not saying that the question of land sovereignty is unimportant, but rather I hope to show that the body (and here, specifically, the post-pornographic body) and its agency, or lack thereof – to fuck, to name, to image – is inextricably connected to sovereign land claims.

The genesis of this book was an attempt to position my own role within neocolonisation in Australia; in particular, how my cultural consumption and production is predicated on and subsumed by colonial narratives. As a white, cisgendered male academic with a research focus in pornography and visual culture, I am seeking to explain the role of pornography as a tool for silencing Indigenous agency and decolonial praxis. The suspension of the Racial Discrimination Act in Australia between 2007–2011 to target Aboriginal communities in *The Northern Territory Emergency Response* was a key moment for the development of this book. Amongst a range of new measures that denied Aboriginal sovereignty was a measure banning pornography in Aboriginal communities. Tracing the history, rationale and findings of this ban uncovered how pornography had become weaponised in neocolonial forms of governmentality. The ban is contingent on a belief in the role of pornography in everyday life, and a paternalistic belief that certain bodies need to be protected from it.[9] This book does not attempt to speak for, or define Indigenous sexual agency, rather it seeks to expose the neocolonial frameworks that distribute pornography under a strict logic of white settlement. In Chapter 1 I reveal this by examining examples of pornography made in settler colonies to define the "colonial porno-exotic" as a form of white immigration propaganda. In Chapter 2 I assess the current global absence of Indigenous pornstars as part of global neocolonial elimination strategies, and in Chapter 3 I propose a theory of the cumshot as a material gesture that authenticates settlers' property claims.

Cum as colonial material

A primary aim of this book is to demonstrate how porn, and its consumption by white male settlers operates as a neocolonial action and structure. I suggest that porn and in particular the cumshot, is not primarily a form of entertainment or release for male settlers, but central to constructing the settler's identity as male, reproductive, white and excessive communal colonial workers. Examining how the cumshot is used, constructed and distributed reveals how it secures cum as both a symbolic and literal material of white futurity.

The cumshot is a product of the pharmacopornographic era – an era that Preciado (2013) defines through mapping the histories of two new industries of the mid twentieth century (pharma and porn) and how they come to dominate the regulation, expression and discipline of gender, sex, desire and sexuality. By the 1970s the cumshot becomes a staple of heteroporn (Ziplow 1977). The most surprising quality of the cumshot is that since its rapid ascension it has remained largely unchanged and central to pornography despite the radical changes to the medium, appearance and distribution of heteroporn over the last 30 years. I claim that the cumshot is an interactive act of heterosex that connects white men through demonstrations of control over bodily material production. The cumshot is a new form of heterosex that supports settler colonisation by maintaining the white male as a productive unit and distributing this explicit productivity into the sensible through what Eldeman (2004, p. 17) terms as 'the logic of reproductive futurism'. The cumshot is both the literal substance of white futurity and a fluid signifier of excessive production. The cumshot is a sex act that draws on different disciplinary and somatic regimes – colonial and neocolonial, biopower and pharmacopornographic, material and representative, industrial and neoliberal – to become part of the quotidian and garbled work of demonstrating ownership on stolen land.

To unpack this claim, the cumshot must first be understood as comprising of "three shootings" – the actor ejaculating, the camera recording and the viewer ejaculating (Aydemir 2007). Because the cumshot is the most explicit of pornographic gestures, the viewer's participation is rarely taken into account, and further, the fact that the actor typically masturbates himself to ejaculation is dismissed. If the cumshot is considered, somewhat counter intuitively, as a sex act that connects white men through masturbation, it opens it up to an operation that is primarily homosocial. That the viewer cums with a male actor and an imagined community of male viewers is disguised in the most "hetero" of representations.[10] This is significant because male masturbation has escaped the critical examination afforded to coupled heterosex. If masturbation is the most common sexual expression for hetero couples, then it should not be dismissed as largely inconsequential to settler sexuality, especially as new forms of masturbation emerge such as the cumshot. For the male settler who masturbates daily, the cumshot is a primary expression of heterosex, it is not lesser than, or a substitute for, coupled heterosex. Partnered heterosex provides the public and critical discourse around heterosexuality, privately it can fail or not even exist while still maintaining its cultural dominance in heteronormativity (Jagose 2013). Masturbation, and in particular male masturbation through the cumshot, satiates the settler's colonial desires and anxieties through social, political and representative networks that protect his privilege and recast that expression as individual, natural and insignificant. My focus is on how the cumshot is directly connected to settler sexuality and settler labour. I argue that it places sex between men as central to settler sexuality in the former and demonstrates bodily exertion that transforms land into property in the latter. The cumshot as settler labour affirms authentic material production, independent from the authenticity of pleasure and orgasm. The cumshot in porn is raw material production and display, and raw material control (of bodies, land, resources) is primarily the work of white men in a settler colony. Therefore, the cumshot is an explicit representation of material work located as coming from within the white male body.

Seeing the cumshot as work places it within settler colonisation's demand for the constant proof of labour. Following Locke (2018), a very restricted definition of labour is used to justify property in settler colonies. For Locke the natural rights to property were only afforded to those who laboured the land in a particular European way. Land without evidence of this labour was considered to be unowned. This prevailing Lockean definition allowed settlers to ignore and deny the sovereignty of Indigenous people, with the violence of *Terra Nullius* in Australia resting on a question of labour. Through Locke, the settler is not an immigrant that supplants existing sovereignty, but one that establishes sovereignty over something that is legally determined incompatible. In a settler colony 'land is remade into property and human relationships to land are restricted to the relationship of the owner to his property. Epistemological, ontological, and cosmological relationships to land are interred, indeed made pre-modern and backward. Made savage' (Tuck and Yang 2012, p. 5). Settler sexuality is an essential part of this process, whereby Indigenous sex and sexualities are constructed as pre-modern and savage, resulting in white settlers structuring their own futurity (heterosexuality) against Indigenous futurity. The racialised incompatibility of settler and Indigenous sexuality turns the sexual violence of colonisation (as well as desires, relationships and children) into issues of assimilation and miscegenation – the process of making white and erasing Indigeneity. The cumshot is a product of the histories of settler sexuality and settler labour.

The settler must constantly prove the land is their property, and the only way to do this is through Lockean work. The colony is defined by the *structures* of work that prove land is property rather than a singular violent *event* of invasion and dispossession (Wolfe 1999, p. 2). Hence settler colonies must be (re)produced every day. Blood, sweat and tears are colonial bodily materials that provide a naturalising nexus between the body of the settler and the land that he labours on. However, as neocolonialism demands new types of labour, and domestic property is increasingly defined by consumption rather than production, a new bodily material attains Lockean status. For Locke labour is 'the work of his hands'.[11] We can apply Locke's definition of labour to the production of semen. Semen is not only produced by the settler's hand but is a colonial product in itself. Whereas blood, sweat and tears are by-products of colonial labour, semen is affirmation of white futurity coming directly from its privileged subject as well as being a product of his labour. If we consider that the settler 'can only make his identity as a settler by making the land produce, and produce excessively' (Tuck and Yang 2012, p. 6) then the cumshot, as an interactive, daily act of colonial material production is an affirmation of his ability to be excessive in a neocolonial context where the land is now non-productive and toxic because of colonial excess.

Masturbating to and with the cumshot is not a hermetic event, but a product of the specific conditions of domestic property. The fact that the cumshot requires a space that the viewer controls, access to technology, knowledge of pornographic systems and time to himself, means that his ejaculation is an expression of these conditions rather than an orgasmic suspension of them. The cumshot does not require transcendent orgasm to be recognised, it is validated through the conditions of viewership and the material ejaculate that is generated. It is neither spectacular nor inauthentic in the typical way representations of sex are understood. It is a signifier of the mundane productivity of the white male body in a settler colony. It is a constant reinforcing to other white men of the centrality of their body, their work and their material production to the success of the colony. This work appears to exist within what is understood as an orgasm suggesting that the orgasm is not the reward/justification for the labour of colonisation but rather the orgasm is another site of work. Aydemir (2007) and

Johnson (1993) note the difference between representations of male and female orgasm in porn, where the male is devoid of fun, undertaking a duty, and focused on bodily spasms that do not in themselves sign pleasure. Men in porn are often referred to as props, as having tools and equipment to do the job (Smith 1988). The audience also does a job, controlling and choreographing their ejaculations with the actor. A miserable or mundane orgasm avoids any radical alterity that an "earthshaking" orgasm might produce. We might consider these orgasms as fake, but as work they are real, connecting men together through material and image-based systems. The colonising white male body is always at work and any pleasure felt is held outside of an economy that is focused on calculating excessive material (re)production. I am interested in how porn structures cum as a material economy, and how this is connected to other representations of colonial work and material production. Understood this way, the cumshot is not closed in a binary relationship to orgasm (biomaterial/affect) but rather opens out, deemphasises the orgasm and connects to a larger representational structure of the ongoing and never-ending work of colonisation.

The first journal dedicated to the study of pornography was launched in 2014, and the first journal of decolonial studies in 2012. These disciplines are still being defined and defended in academia, with the questions they raise causing controversies that upset the justifications and logics that maintain scholarly institutions. While these new disciplines raise separate questions, they intersect and contribute to each other in approach, method and pedagogy. Their mere presence is at once a threat to other disciplines, as well as under threat of disciplinary exclusion. This book examines some of these intersections, in order to show how pornography is structured according to a Native/non-Native binary, and how settler colonisation has used pornography as a technics of settler sexuality. This book is not simply a call to decolonise pornography, but to demonstrate how analytic curiosity towards pornography can lead us towards decolonial questions, and inversely, how pornographising decolonial discourse may contribute new tactics towards Indigenous sovereignty and futurity.

Notes

1 Of course, pornography was produced and consumed by the working and middle class. These alternate and mostly erased histories of various pornographies do not inform cotemporary heteroporn due to their different mediums, technologies and distribution. Contemporary heteroporn can be

traced to the protected archives of "erotic" art and photography (such as the sealed porn collected in the Russian State Library, founded in the 1920s) which became more distributed as the twentieth century progressed.
2 The Australian Bureau of Statistics inadvertently reveals the hollowness of naturalised terms like "households", ultimately defining it through food: 'each occupant who usually supplies his/her own food should be counted as a separate household' (Australian Bureau of Statistics 2003). Under this definition the fridge can be seen as the determining factor of a household, holding the food of occupants who become a household though a lack of accounting. While in practice this definition is used for group housing, it demonstrates the vagueness around significant normative terms.
3 This is seen in the infamous case of Henrietta Lacks, and the non-consensual harvesting of her cells in the 1951. The continued use of her cells, long after her death, demonstrates how the Black body is the literal material of medical research which is commodified, patented and profited from.
4 This does not include white male bodies in heteroporn, as their representation is taken for granted, as a structural necessity for the appearance of the true pornographic subject. Although, as Chapter 3 will argue, the structurally necessary white male in heteroporn may be more than simply a scaffold for the action.
5 This meme refers to Lynndie England, a United States Army Reserve solider who posed for photographs smiling and pointing during the torture and abuse of prisoners at Abu Ghraib prison in Baghdad in 2003. It is significant because photography was used as a specific torture technique by US soldiers during their occupation of Iraq.
6 This is part of Clark's testimony for Lord Longford's 1972 report on pornography. Clark, an art historian, was invested in defining pornography to defend the value of art and preserve a space for pornography in art according to his own standards of literal taste – he goes on to define porn as a 'too strong flavour' added to a dish.
7 Perhaps this is really to say that any critics of my work are in a very real sense, wankers.
8 As Veracini (2013, p. 313) claims, 'settler colonial phenomena ... are inherently transnational and transcultural'.
9 Then Australian Federal Health Minister, Tony Abbott, called for a 'new paternalism' (Metherell 2006) to combat what he saw as rampant sexual abuse in Aboriginal communities.
10 This imagined community is also very real, as most online porn platforms features the exact number of views. The viewer becomes part of that community, their view added to the number despite the disguise of private browsing.
11 In Locke's *Second Treastse on Civil Government* (2018, para. 27), he states 'The Labour of his Body, and the Work of his Hands, we may say, are properly his'.

1 Colonial pornographic exotica

Pornography produced within settler colonies is part of broader cultural strategies that identify what types of bodies are allowed to live and reproduce. All settler colonies have an anxious relationship to population as both the elimination of Indigenous people and the rapid growth of the colonial population is required (Wolfe 2006). These two objectives are never independent, however the narratives, law and politics of a settler colony holds them as separate tasks.[1] Colonial cultural practices predominantly focus on the growth of the population by weaving it into narratives of survival, triumph and nationalism. The elimination of Indigenous populations, on the rare occasions that it is depicted, suggest it is the cause of colonisation in an abstract sense (as a symbol of modernity) but never directly attributable to any particular act of colonial violence or colonial strategy. In the eyes of colonisers, Indigenous subjects are assumed to either be already dead or belonging to the past and so in the process of dying. Pornography is the most direct cultural signifier of population growth, as it is the only cultural form that can explicitly depict bodies fucking. The decisions of who, where, why and how often bodies fuck are pedagogic devices in settler pornography. This chapter focuses on Australian heteroporn to unpack the operation of these pedagogic strategies, in particular, it focuses on the development of the "pornoexotic" (the exoticisation of heterosex). The Australian pornoexotic is made for an international audience, functioning as advertising for white migration. It depicts a land of, and for, white people, in which the expansionist demands of the colony result in excessive sexual proclivity. Excessive sexual activity and desire is portrayed as constructive rather than disruptive, deviant or problematic. The pornoexotic transforms the exceptionality of pornography into a national narrative by conflating explicit sex with white reproductive futurity and the domestication of difference.

Australian heteroporn projects how the colony wants to be seen, and how it sees itself. I examine this through four heteroporn feature films – John T. Bone's *Lost in Paradise* (1991), Pierre Woodman's *The Fugitive 2* (2000), anon.'s *Victoria Blue* (1999) and Aja's *Outback Assignment* (1991). These films imagine Australia as strange and familiar, accessible and distant, licentious and structured according to Western morality. This flattens difference to contrived locational, symbolic and racial exotic cues, and "naturalises" settler sexuality and desire. In the films examined this is achieved by activating "Australianness" appropriated from pre-existing media representations, through the role of the outsider protagonist who acts as witness and judge of the exotic fiction, and through homosociality disguised as mateship. This chapter focuses on this explicit vision as the first part of the operation of pornography in a settler colony. Chapter 2 focuses on the less visible but just as important second part – the extinction narrative, which deliberately removes Indigenous people from cultural representations of sexual agency, desire and reproduction.

The pornoexotic

In an expanded sense, the term pornoexotic refers to any means by which pornographic content is distanced from its intended viewer. This is most commonly achieved by activating stereotypes of race, class and geography to signify to the viewer that what they are witnessing is not part of their community. The pornoexotic has links with the larger category of exotic representations, which commonly allude to fantasies of sexual licentiousness and deviancy. We can clearly locate exotic erotica as part of the representational system of colonisation. As Pease (2000, p. 128) states,

> The exotic lies outside the restrictive operations of classical rules and opens up an entirely unexplored imaginative region. Pornographic notions of the Orient, just as hegemonic cultural notions, do not necessarily reflect any specific reality of the Orient, but, as Edward Said has suggested, do reflect a particular European definition of itself as contrasting image, idea, and experience to its exoticized other.

The exotic is a spectacle that generates curiosity, and in doing so excuses the viewer for the act of viewing. For Said (1993, p. 159) 'the exotic replaces the impress of power with the blandishments of curiosity', which is often represented in depictions of the 'unrestrained sexuality' of non-Europeans (Nead 1990, p. 332).[2] While the exotic and the Oriental should not be conflated, they both manipulate the politics of representation of an unknown other for an ignorant audience. Such representations focus on recently, or yet to be, colonised people and act on an audience who are 'aroused at signs of empire' (Waugh 1996, p. 298).

Orientalist paintings are the dominant example of the eroticisation of the exotic. The distinction Foucault (1978) makes between *scientia sexualis* and *ars erotica* describes how the West saw itself in opposition to the East. In Eastern cultures (*ars erotica*):

> truth is drawn from pleasure itself, understood as a practice and accumulated as experience, pleasure is not considered in relation to an absolute law of the permitted and the forbidden, nor by reference to a criterion of utility, but first and foremost in relation to itself.
>
> (Foucault 1978, p. 57)

The Orientalist paintings of Ingres, Gerome and Delacroix generated a loophole for soft-core pornography to be seen in France. Through heavy Oriental coding, these paintings were at once spectacular and pedagogic. They work to produce arousal at the sign of empire – both the vanquished empire represented by crumbling mosaic arabesque and looted interiors, and the powerful French empire reporting back the depravity it encountered. Yet as has been extensively discussed in the disciplines of art history and postcolonial theory, Orientalist representations are nothing more than the fantasy of the West, with many of these artists never having travelled to the regions they depict.

Apparent in these paintings are racial hierarchies that place white (female) bodies as the object of eroticisation. Although typically in the position of a slave or sex worker, the white female is commonly attended to by people of colour. It is clear how these paintings can be considered both pornography and propaganda at the same time – they are both spectacular and explicit, and imbued with the racial logics of colonialism. Indeed, Orientalist exhibitions in metropoles were hugely popular, particularly with women. This may seem strange, especially as the pedagogic intent was to warn women of the dangers of being unchaperoned in public (the unfounded fear of a white sex slave trade was, and still is, a constant theme). The eroticisation of the exotic produced what Nash (2014, p. 3) describes as 'complex and unnerving pleasures'. Somewhat paradoxically, Orientalism became one of the few sexual outlets for women by depicting fantasies of lesbianism and interracial sex that suggested the possibilities of pleasure outside of heteronormativity. However, these deviations from heteronormativity were always focused on the white body, specifically the exposed female or the voyeuristic male (most famously in Jean-Auguste-Dominique Ingre's *Le Bain Turk* 1863, where the audience is the voyeur looking through the 'keyhole'). In such works, the focus remains on the colonial white body but the background changes, providing the necessary distance to excuse their promiscuity, while making certain that erotic agency is never projected onto non-white bodies. In this way the normative/colonial is the explicit measure of deviance/otherness; that is, the normative "deviation" of white sexuality is the only allowable representation of otherness.

Throughout the nineteenth and twentieth centuries different approaches achieved the same end. For example, Picasso's Cubist paintings were directly influenced by the colonial spoils contained in The Musée d'Ethnographie du Trocadéro. His depiction of prostitutes in *Les Demoiselles d'Avignon* (1907), clearly references the conventions of pornography, with the subjects looking directly at the viewer who is no longer a voyeur but is implicated in the act of looking. This pornographic gaze in art history has been classified as "naked", meaning the subject is aware of being looked at; the nude is more distant, as the subject is ignorant of the viewer (Berger 2008). Orientalist paintings are nudes, whereas Picasso's models are naked. The danger with naked bodies is that the viewer cannot be excused for their gaze, as it is explicitly for them. Orientalist paintings had to be nudes, for it was not only the viewer but the process of colonisation itself which was at risk of being implicated in the "depravity" depicted if the gaze was returned. Their status as public (and hence erotic not pornographic) required the careful navigation of symbolism and composition to ensure that their integration into the sensible (art history) avoided discussing their domestic appeal and use. *Les Demoiselles d'Avignon* is not distanced geographically, as the location is identified in the title. Rather, the exoticisation is achieved through the style and subject. The distorted and flattened perspective, the appropriation of masks from Gabon, Cameroon and Equatorial Guinea, and the blocks of colour with heavy outline are signs to the audience to read the work as carrying a "primitive" representative power. The white women are able to be stylistically depicted as "savages" who can be feared and desired because they are sex workers. They are made savage through Picasso's use of colonial symbolism. This deliberately connects the public exposure of sex workers to the colonial framing of Native sex and nudity as always already public and hence available to the coloniser. In all the above examples, racial and cultural cues are employed to distance and excuse the viewer while maintaining the spectacular and arousing content fixed on white bodies. Held in the rubric of contemplation rather than masturbation, Orientalist and Modernist paintings were unproblematically integrated into the cannon as depictions (documents, diagnostics, experiments) of *ars erotica* by *scientia sexualis* artists.

The pornoexotic has a less visible history alongside erotic art, with nineteenth century examples of pornographic photography using Oriental props to signify distance. There are examples of these signifiers being painted on top of pornographic photographs. In these we see the literal superficial layering of exotic symbols over the white female pornographic body. The fiction of distance placed on top of an otherwise heteronormative image is precisely how the pornoexotic operates – the two layers have no relation to one another; in other words, there is no interaction, hybridity, diffusion, infection or conversation. The pornoexotic is a subcategory of heteroporn that sits between pornography and exotica. Because of this, the pornoexotic also inhabits a space between public and domestic as it relies on references to non-pornographic representational systems and symbols to be understood. Pornoexotica differs from standard heteroporn because of its reliance on these public symbols of exotica that signify geographic distance. Morris and Paasonen (2014, p. 226) argue that 'porn is about place being dominated by flesh … In porn, space is deflated by the fascinating presence and actions of bodies'. However, in pornoexotica the recognition of place *allows* the fascination of the audience without judgement (internal or public) for its prurient fascination. The pornoexotic can afford to be more openly unexceptional because of this conservative distancing of the pornographic. The circular logic of the pornoexotic activates stereotypes of racial and cultural difference to distance pornography from the audience, yet these same sexualised stereotypes connect the audience's desires and domestic use of pornography to their public participation in, and maintenance of, exclusion based on difference. Pornography and difference are tied together in the pornoexotic in ways that reveal, and are part of, the systemic sexual violence of colonisation.

The pornoexotic is one of the most popular genres of professional pornography. While there are a variety of reasons for the genre's popularity, a notable factor is that in the United States, during the 1960s and 1970s, "foreign films" were often code for pornography. Distributors like Radley Metzger imported European pornographic films as a way to get around censorship laws and show white bodies that were also exotic (playing on the stereotype that Europeans were more sexually exploratory than the puritan United States). Sexploitation films like these continue today, typically set in Eastern European countries where an "outsider" with American dollars or euros is able to buy sex from anyone they encounter. Contemporary pornoexotica represents economic imperialism as the power to make anyone a willing sex worker. Operating in a late capitalist context, the audience's arousal is drawn from displays of particular currencies as new signs of empire.

The most commercially successful pornographic feature film of all time, *Pirates* (Joone 2005), is a clear example of pornoexotica.[3] It is an interesting example of the pornoexotic that distances the viewer in time and place because it is set in a generalised, non-specific Caribbean and in a generic mythical sense of time. *Pirates* does not take place here and now, but it also does not take place specifically there and then. It uses the pirate as the exotic, immoral other who resists, yet is a symptom of, colonial expansion. The pirate, as a generic fantasy of depravity and of a lost age, is the perfect pornoexotic character as it allows for the "unwilling" female actors and the male pirates to all be white without disrupting the exotic context. However, *Pirates'* ultimate success was because of its reliance on Disney's *Pirates of the Caribbean* franchise, which was launched in 2003. *Pirates* promised what the Hollywood films could not, a pornographic closure of the exotic narrative. Unlike countless of other pornographic spoof films, *Pirates* was a pornographic film built on, and extending, the cinematic fantasy of *Pirates of the Caribbean*. The representation of sex in cinema is necessarily distanced because fucking cannot be shown. As Žižek (1992, pp. 110–11) demonstrates, there are different ways cinema distances sex – from humour to symbolism to direct manipulation of the fantasy. This suggests that the 'congruence between the filmic narrative (the unfolding of the story) and the immediate display of the sexual act, is structurally impossible'. For Žižek, the pornographic and the filmic narrative are mutually exclusive. Yet the pornoexotic contests this – instead of distancing the representation of sex it distances the audience through filmic narrative. For this strategy to be successful the narrative must operate alongside the fucking and, even in its tokenistic, humorous and stilted manner, must be invested in. This narrative is reinforced and made serious through the use of easily recognisable cultural references (as *Pirates* did). The pornoexotic demonstrates how pornography is structurally connected to filmic and social narrative. This is not widely understood or accepted because it is assumed that when the fucking starts the narrative is 'no longer taken seriously and starts to function only as pretext for introducing acts of copulation' (Žižek 1992, p. 111). The pornoexotic's reliance on narrative, a narrative that is not opposed to the fucking, shows us that porn is *primarily* filmic, social and political. The opposition that Žižek sets up naturalises sex in porn and ultimately naturalises the colonial narratives that structure the fucking. If we start with the narrative and analyse towards the sex, rather than the inverse, we avoid this opposition and can denaturalise both porn's narratives and explicitness.

The indexical power of pornography (that it is what it depicts) applies to the fucking and narrative symbolism. This was seen when *Pirates* was refused classification in Australia because of a CGI scene of two skeletons fighting (Stardust 2014). The classification of pornography does not allow violence of any type (even violence that would otherwise be allowed in a G rating), presumably for fear that representations of violence will produce actual violence in the audience. In other words, both the fucking and the narrative are assumed to be consumed by the audience as real rather than phantasma – even in the case of CGI skeletons. The inverse, that the fucking could be read as phantasma, was not something the classification board considered. Despite the refusal of classification, *Pirates'* success was due to the fact that it was both conservative heteroporn and a film that could be talked about (or alluded to) in public as a *film*. The pornoexotic more readily enters public discussion than other forms of pornography. As I argued in the Introduction, the paradox of pornography is that it is not exceptional and yet trades on exceptionality. The pornoexotic is the most easily identifiable non-exceptional pornographic genre. It can be more openly non-exceptional because the fucking takes place "a long time ago, in a galaxy far away" (as *Porn Wars* attests). The pornoexotic suggests that fucking can be read as both phantasmic *and* real (as a process of naturalising fantasies). I argue that pornography deliberately absorbs explicit fucking into narrative and into broader non-pornographic representational systems.

Fantasy pornoexotic films like *Pirates* operate in their own appropriated universe. However, when the pornoexotic uses and references real locations with histories of colonisation, the integration of the pornographic into the exotic presents the possibility for the exotic myth to be disrupted by the explicit fucking of the other. The colonial pornoexotic is the opposite of Orientalist erotica as it is produced in the colony, rather than being a mise-en-scène of the exotic produced in the metropole. This opens up a moment in which the fantasies of the oppressor, the outsider and the tourist are confronted with an image that cannot sustain its own characterisation. In order to mitigate this, the colonial pornoexotic rhetorically references the other for salacious effect, but at the same time ensures that it remains symbolic – that is, unfuckable. Genre expectations combined with exotic narratives of subjugated difference could potentially destabilise the modalities of viewership. In other words, because the pornoexotic contains the pornographic it must prove that the exotic is a facade, not only to align with the normative desires of its audience, but also to prevent the possibility that it might accidentally represent the very sexual oppression that the exotic masks as erotic. The exotic is paused so that heteroporn can sit on top of it. This is an inversion of the pornographic photographs of white bodies taken in studios in France with Orientalist symbols painted on top. In colonial pornoexotica, the white body is always placed over a paused exotic (land, culture, community and so on). Colonial pornoexotica takes a more conservative approach than Orientalism to ensure racial boundaries are maintained and that the settler's desires are ignited by *place* but only satisfied through other settlers.

The Australian pornoexotic

Australia functions as an appropriate site for what Said terms the 'domestication of the exotic' (Said 1994, p. 60). Since British invasion, Australia has been paradoxically perceived as an alien, harsh environment that would absorb problematic elements of English society *and* as a readily tamed landscape for the replication of England (Gould 2011). Contemporary Australia, as an exotic location, is an exemplar of Paul Theroux's (1986) notion of "home-plus", where the landscape offers the spectacular "plus" while the ongoing process of settler colonialism ensures a comfortable, non-threatening "home" experience for Western tourists/immigrants. When Australia is used as the location for narrative pornographic films it draws on the comfortable exotic, overlaid with the hypersexualisation of white bodies. All settler colonies have different imagined exotic characteristics, and Australia's exotica is the landscape, the animals and distance, which provide a physical and existential "threat" to Western bodies and culture that requires (pornographic) maintenance.

The characteristics of the Australian pornoexotic are largely directed at global audiences, and the films examined here were produced by non-Australian companies for an international audience. They were, however, sold in Australia and local audiences may have a similar response to global audiences as for white Australians the notion that the land is both exotic and familiar is central to the fantasy of a settler state. The pornoexotic is for the occident, generated by demand for salacious representations of imperial success. White Australian audiences either suspend their own position through racial rather than national identification or view it with a mixture of pride and/or irony because of their lack of distance to the fiction presented.

It is interesting to note that there are a variety of factors that make these films more targeted to international audiences beyond the fact that the colonial pornoexotic is designed and produced in the periphery by metropoles. Stardust's (2014) examination of the Australian pornographic industry reveals the financial and legal complexities for contemporary production. One of the key restrictions is that it is only legal to produce pornography in the Australian Capital Territory.[4] The pornoexotic relies on recognisable symbols of the exotic (landscape, people, icons), however, if porn producers included icons such as the Sydney Opera House, they would open themselves up to prosecution. As such, contemporary porn producers often shoot in spaces that cannot be identified to avoid the expense of shooting in the Australian Capital Territory (Stardust 2014, p. 251). It is not only the production that is restricted. Censorship laws, as well as the cost of classification, prevent much of the material produced in Australia being accessible to local audiences. This means that local production is restricted to small, amateur, micro-budget films. Recent feature style porn produced in Australia, such as Michelle Flynn's *Momentum Vol 1–4* (2014–2016), has been screened internationally at film festivals yet remains difficult to access for domestic audiences. It is for these practical reasons that the Australian pornoexotic is predominantly targeted to global audiences.[5] The films studied here were produced in a more open environment (or more correctly at a time when the industry was under less scrutiny) and hence could use the landscape more explicitly. It is for this reason they were chosen for study. While these films are all more than 15 years old, they remain relevant to ongoing neocolonial measures in Australia. Furthermore, the disruption of the internet and the general demise of high budget pornographic films is another cause of the decline in feature length colonial pornoexotica. The cost of sending out a crew to Australia is prohibitive for porn production. It is far easier, as *Hustler* did in *The Cougar Hunter* (Morgan 2009), to shoot in America and use props to signify Australia.

I am focusing on colonial heteroporn as it most directly displays anxious white reproductive futurity. There is a parallel history of gay porn that is surprisingly similar to the examples analysed here. Gay pornoexotica uses the same signifiers of the exotic; that is, the same emphasis on the landscape and fascination with fit white bodies. Alan McKee's (1999) study of these Australian gay porn films refers to them as displaying 'desperate nationalism'. This is a good description of Australian pornoexotic, both gay and straight, as it projects a histrionic nationalism that would be familiar to domestic audiences who watch any Australian content aimed at a global audience. McKee claims that there is a difference for domestic audiences watching gay pornoexotica, namely that it affirms gay sex as existing in Australia. For colonial heteroporn films such a local identification is not radical and instead provides an explicit pedagogic image of white reproductive futurity. I do not want to conflate gay and straight pornoexotica, nor conflate homo and heteronormativity. While there are commonalities, there are also important differences. For instance, sex between men is a particular (unacknowledged) characteristic of Australian colonisation. While similar sex acts between men in both gay and straight pornoexotica exist, the institution of mateship separates homosociality from homosexuality. But beyond sexual identitarian politics, national masculinity remains stable across both gay and straight examples – sex is encouraged to be shared between white men.

The Australian pornoexotic can be identified through four key features. First, a generic, recognisable "Australianness", appropriated from pre-existing media representations and deployed to ensure the audience can readily locate the exotic narrative. Second, the dominance of the landscape, and at times fauna, provide the catalyst for action, marking the scene as a site of exception where participants become corrupted and thus excused for their behaviour. Third, the presence of a protagonist "outsider" – a surrogate for the audience and the proto-migrant – whose journey transforms their fear of difference into the domestic platitudes of white heteronormative desire. Last, the Australian pornoexotic is recognised through homosociality, sex between straight men as a bonding experience of mateship. The promise or presence of a woman is required, but she becomes the object through which mateship can be experienced and through which the outsider is accepted. While these are the visible characteristics of the Australian pornoexotic, the most important invisible characteristic in these films is the negotiation of race, notably the absence of Aboriginal people. This absence is the subject of Chapter 2.

Exotic landscape/generic Australianness

The Australia portrayed in the films relies on established signifiers. The films reinforce these signifiers, presumably to align with their primary audience's expectations. Pleasure is derived simply from recognising the easily identifiable signifiers of the exotic itself (Shimizu 2007).[6] The pleasure comes from the feeling of mastery over difference, as there is an important distinction between recognisable difference and actual difference. Actual difference is not "recognisable" because it sits outside of known representational frameworks, whereas recognisable difference always denotes a power relation. Representations of the exotic are hence always experienced as difference that has been subjugated (translated, captioned, ordered). This can also be understood through Rancière's distribution of the sensible – that the representation becomes recognisable through the violence of making it legible to the system that produced the conditions in the first place. As Solomon-Godeau (1991, p. 176) states, it is 'a double act of subjugation: first, in the social world that has produced its victims; and second, in the regime of the image produced within and for the same system that engenders the conditions it then represents'. The Australia that is represented is the already colonised land, which is why it is legible.

In the case of colonial pornoexotica, the representation of Australia mimics the stereotypes established by globally successful films and associated advertising campaigns. For instance, references to *Crocodile Dundee* (Faiman 1986) are implicitly and explicitly present in the Australian pornoexotica. In *Crocodile Dundee* an American outsider is sent to Australia on a reporting assignment and falls in love with Michael "Crocodile" Dundee, a rugged, taciturn "Aussie" with a connection to wild animals, played by Paul Hogan. The four pornoexotic films follow a similar narrative of an outsider forced to adapt to the Australian environment. *The Fugitive 2* features a Crocodile Dundee-like character who feeds crocodiles and is referred to as their friend. Paul Hogan, the actor who played the character of Crocodile Dundee, was used in the 'Come and Say G'day' advertising campaign by Tourism Australia in the 1980s, marking the culmination of iterative international media images of Australia that started in the 1960s (Crawford 2010). The campaign solidified 'a picture of

Australians as mostly white, blonde, and either on a beach or in a pub' (Khamis 2012, p. 60). It is not surprising, then, that in the 1990s Australian pornoexotica drew heavily from the narrative and imagery in this campaign.

In Tourism Australia's advertisements, the beach is the site where the exotic is eroticised. As Moreton-Robinson (2015, 2018) argues, the beach is the key site for performances of white possession. Unlike the pub or the bush, the beach is reserved for young, athletic, white people, and in tourism images is typically depicted as deserted, except for the few affable figures that match this stereotype. The isolation hints at salacious activities permitted (or at least possible) in this space but, crucially, this sexualised Australia is sold as belonging only to white bodies. The exotic elements in these beach scenes are reduced to an unproblematic, depoliticised and "ancient" landscape. Precisely because the landscape is considered in this way, it has the effect of 'naturalizing and affirming dominant narratives of history, identity and entitlement' (Lukinbeal 2005, p. 13). The exotic landscape is available exclusively to white bodies, and this becomes the ideological justification that allows for total racial segregation without critique.[7] The "ancient" landscape, and by implication, Aboriginal people are "naturally" segregated from colonisation because they are fundamentally incompatible. As such, colonisation is separated from dispossession, which works to affirm a white possessive logic. This is most obvious in the Tourism Australia campaign that starred Lara Bingle (an Australian model and media personality) in 2006. The final shot shows Bingle walking out of the ocean onto a totally deserted beach, as she looks directly to camera and says, 'Where the bloody hell are you?' This gonzo-style address to the audience underlines exactly who is entitled to the eroticised exotic.

These various neocolonial representational strategies in pornography and advertising acknowledge the existence of otherness, only to show it in the service of the Western gaze. As Shimizu (2007, p. 108) states, the other is a 'being-for-others, specifically for the white male author and spectator'. The other has no value until it is subjected to Western judgement. In the Lara Bingle campaign, this is alluded to when an Aboriginal dancer says to camera, 'We've been rehearsing for 40,000 years'. Here the other exists as a rehearsal, as an incomplete space until it is contrasted by white heteronormativity – the body of the coloniser, the tourist, the pornstar. This is a clear example of a cultural practice "waiting" to be distributed into the sensible, as though until the point of colonial distribution it has no agency and no visibility. "Rehearsal" is a particularly cruel term, as it suggests an awareness and preparation for the coming event of (neo)colonisation. Rehearsal means that Aboriginal agency could only be completed by the coloniser – by the 'white male author and spectator'. This is how colonised land and people can be both fundamentally incompatible (as an impossible difference unable to be represented) and always already completely integrated into colonisation (rehearsing before invasion).

The prevalence of this representation of Australia shows no signs of dissipating. In 2018, Tourism Australia ran an advertisement during the NFL Super Bowl that not only reinforced these stereotypes but used the exact same symbols from the 1980s campaign. Based on the release of a fake film, *Dundee Returns*, it shows the story of an outsider's (Dundee's son) uncomfortable appearance in the outback through restaging iconic scenes from the original films. He is told about the '37,000 miles of pristine beach mate' over a helicopter shot of an empty beach before being given the "homeplus" tour of Australia, which is full of the 'finest wines' and 'world class restaurants'. It finishes with a cameo of Paul Hogan and a tautology, 'you are the best Crocodile Dundee since Crocodile Dundee'. The advert exists entirely in an insular system of representations, not only of filmic references but also of Tourism Australia's own advertisements. The unwillingness to show anything remotely outside of the 1980s version of Australia suggests that, if anything, the Australian exotic is becoming more restricted to these stereotypes. The problematic Lara Bingle campaign at least had representations of Aboriginal people and women – neither of which make an appearance in the 2018 campaign. We are witnessing a return to a particular notion of white masculine mateship as the only identity through which Australia can be understood and experienced. The advert ends with three Crocodile Dundees (the old, the new, the tourist) as if their (parthenogenetic) reproduction through mateship is the goal of the settler nation.

The Australian pornoexotic amplifies these existing representations and closes the narrative by explicitly depicting Australia as full of sexually available, uninhibited white women (and men). As McKee (1999, p. 195) notes of gay Australian pornoexotic films from the 1990s, 'these porn videos offer nothing about being Australian other than the fact that they are made in something which is already called Australia'. We see only the Australia we expect to see in these films, but when combined with explicit sex they reveal unique operations of neocolonisation.

Imposition of landscape

The landscape is the primary element of the Australian pornoexotic, and as such, its influence is amplified. This is because it performs its role without necessitating the appearance of different bodies or desires, "easily" accommodating white heteronormativity. The "strangeness" of the empty landscape is the exotic backdrop that allows transgression to occur outside, offering an uninterrupted view for the audience. The landscape is outdoors, but is not strictly classified as private or public, so a different type of voyeurism occurs, we stumble across the fucking which is part of the composition of an exotic landscape. More precisely, it is land that is under colonial rule but does not have the signifiers of colonial labour. Sex, in this space, does not belong to a specific settler but to all settlers and future settlers. It can draw on the exotic, safe to expose the white body in a space that is protected by colonial rule. Yet because the landscape must be fucked in (or "on"), there are moments that the tourist image is disrupted by the absurdity of white bodies engaged in heterosex in remote Australian environments. The pornoexotic has to go further than the exotic, providing explicit proof of the completion of the fantasy through the imprint of fucking being left on the landscape. At times this results in a reverse movement of the landscape leaving an imprint on the actors. It is in these unintentional reversals that the landscape speaks back, asserting a counternarrative that ruptures the pornographic one. It disrupts the "silent" and "ancient" land by showing its inhospitality, or indifference, to the fucking. In non-porn Australian films this inhospitable quality is a common trope, to be overcome through struggle. In porn, an assumed synergy between white heterosex and nature is at odds with adversity narratives, and so the struggle to fuck has to be hidden, otherwise it could be read as the work of, rather than the reward for, colonisation.

The problem the landscape sets up in these films – to be, at once, the vehicle that allows for sexual encounters to occur and an intrusive element that unintentionally disrupts the sex scene – is negotiated in a variety of disjointed ways. In *Lost in Paradise*, an aviary provides the backdrop for a male/female sex scene. The couple walk into the aviary, which has sweeping views over a pastoral landscape. As they start to kiss, a bird lands on the woman's head, breaking the performance for a moment. Then the man reaches out and removes the bird while she laughs uncomfortably. The resultant scene is constantly interrupted with shadows of birds flying overhead, a peacock pacing in the background, and the sounds of squawks and the flapping of wings. The scene concludes with the predictable shot of the man's cum face. Without pausing, the camera pans upwards to reveal two sulphur-crested cockatoos sitting just above his head. The deliberate use of Australian birds and other exotic birds in the scene denotes the "paradise" of a polyamorous community the protagonist discovers. It suggests a type of commune, a cornucopia of flora and fauna beyond species differentiation. It is reminiscent of the many Orientalist paintings, epitomised by artists like Paul Gauguin, that display a flattening of landscape, people and animals (Duran 2009). There is a type of immediacy and intimacy that occurs across these planes – a romanticisation of the exotic person's affinity with, and mystic knowledge of, the landscape and animals. Crucially the exotic people in these films are always colonisers, not Indigenous people, who have become exotic because they live in an exotic landscape. The outsider (both the audience and the tourist) may feel drawn into this connection, fooling themselves of the authenticity of their own fantasy. Underpinning all of this is the belief that the exotic landscape has the power to transform lives, and that this transformational power can have an attenuated effect on the audience who only experiences the exotic through representations (Stadler and Mitchell 2010). The intention of the scene is to unleash the exotic within the visitor, linking ancient mysticism with settler desire. The actors are transformed/perverted from their normal lives into animalistic desiring bodies. However, the scene fails to smoothly incorporate "nature" into heterosex, ultimately only demonstrating Said's notion of the 'domestication of the exotic' – the birds are caged, habituated to human contact, and generically exotic (many are not actually native to Australia).

A more interesting failure occurs during the sex scene. As Lehman (1999, p. 362) maintains in porn 'we watch the actors not the character fucking', there is a moment that characterisation is erased by the reality of bodies fucking. While this is observable throughout *Lost in Paradise* when the thin veneer of characterisation crumbles during the sex scenes, something additional occurs in the aviary scene. The characters dissolve, and to some extent the actors are made more visible because of the presence of the birds (such as the moment of the bird landing on the woman's head), but the fucking itself takes on a different characterisation. While the actors may be exposed, what is actually made visible is cultural, not biological – we see the actor as they struggle to fuck. The animals' indifference, and at times hostility throughout the scene prevents any bestial revelation. There is no moment when the performance breaks down and the fucking ignites a natural, cross-species recognition. The animals respond in the same way to fucking as they do to the camera – there is no differentiation made between the tool and subject of representation. They are an obstacle to heterosex rather than a catalysis. The intention of the imposition of the landscape is clear in this scene – the humans enter a menagerie, placing themselves with, and as, wild animals. However, the failure of this scene reveals the problem of the pornoexotic as opposed to the exotic, which is namely that the latter avoids escaping the myth while the former necessitates moments in which the myth is touched. Because of these breaks the pornoexotic tends to get closer to the subject it mythologises and unintentionally raises questions as to the assumed universality of pornographic representations, which is to say the "naturalness" of the settler body and settler sexuality.

The foregrounding of the background literally occurs in *Outback Assignment*. It produces the most unintentionally comic moment in the film. A commercial photographer is sent to Australia for a series of photoshoots with exotic backdrops. One backdrop is the archetypical deserted beach. What seems like a generic beach is interrupted by a mob of kangaroos. They interact with the actors, getting in the way of the shoot, pulling attention from the semi-naked models attempting to strike poses on the sand. Before long the scene descends into chaos, as the inquisitive animals disrupt the flimsy pretext for the scene and its pornographic intent. The scene is such a failure that it remains in the film as a series of very fast jump cuts, presumably because only a few seconds of footage was usable in each take. The most revealing shot is when a kangaroo hops in front of the camera, taking up half the screen. The camera remains focused on the model posed in the background, but the kangaroo obscures the view, insistently placing itself in the foreground and demanding to be filmed.

How the mob of kangaroos behave in this sequence reveals the "life" of an exotic symbol. The kangaroo has been completely colonised, turned into a symbol on the Australian coat of arms. The difference between this scene and the aviary scene is that there is no cage. The truth of the kangaroo is that their entire existence is within a cage, a cage of law and nationalism, for which they are the non-consenting symbol. If the birds in the aviary respond to the fucking and the camera in the same disinterested way, the kangaroos take this one step further, performing for the camera and becoming the stars. What this scene shows is that the exotic can only exist in already colonised land, and what it finds there is already domesticated difference; that is, forced habituation to the coloniser's gaze.

The exotic that Gauguin found in Tahiti was already "tainted" by Christian missions and European trade. Gauguin was disappointed but this disappointment did not stop him from enjoying himself and turning the effects of violent colonial subjugation into symbols of the exotic. This misrepresentation of colonial effects as pre-colonial exotica is central to how exotica is represented and enjoyed. The kangaroo jumping "naively" in front of the camera would have been very successful as exotica, but it fails as pornoexotica because their physical proximity to the actors and camera prevents the fucking. As symbols they allow white bodies to fuck, but when performing their own survival strategies of habituation, they interrupt the very fucking they inspired. By placing themselves in front of the colonial gaze they are allowed to live (or given the possibility of life) – but when the actual work of colonial sex takes place their existence is superfluous, annoying and even threatening. The use of the kangaroo as a symbol that allows for fucking is more carefully integrated into *The Fugitive 2*. In the final hardcore scene, shot in red sand with Uluru in the background, a jump cut interrupts the middle of the scene. The cut is to a solitary kangaroo bounding across the desert, before cutting back to the hardcore action. The kangaroo is nowhere to be seen around the actors, but is absurdly, and almost subliminally, inserted into the sex scene.

The active role of the landscape is central to *Victoria Blue*, where a leitmotif of a seashell is used as a mythical object that teleports sexual encounters to the protagonist, Gabor. The film opens in a similar manner to all the films studied here; there are wide shots of uninhabited landscapes and a voiceover referring to the location as the 'dreaded skeleton coast of wrecked ships'. The protagonist has travelled from Hungary to South Australia because 'it was as far away as he could get to forget a woman'. The physical distance combined with the strange (yet familiar) landscape provides the setting for taboo sexual encounters. The familiarity he discovers is emphasised in a split-screen scene that compares and contrasts shots from Australia and Hungary, with the voiceover referring to them as 'like strange twins'. Away from his friends and family, and away from his heteronormative dreams of 'a woman', he is freed from sexual conventions. *Victoria Blue* features the most fetishistic practices of the films studied here. It conforms to a script of the exotic as 'contain[ing] sadomasochistic tastes … a fascination with the macabre, notion of the fatal woman, with secrecy and occultism' (Said 1994, p. 180). The extensive set-up at the start of the film generates a space in which blurring between straight and gay, fetish and normative are deemed acceptable because of the occult spell that blurs reality and hallucination. The seashell transports him to sexual scenes, or transports others to him. This plot device solves two problems: the first is that in order to maintain the landscape as empty and wild, his encounters cannot be with people he meets, as this would undo the solitude of his existence, the second is that it places the sex acts in between fiction and reality. Because they are real and fake (no clear indication is ever given if the seashell is actually magical, or if he is fantasising), fetishistic practices are presented as symptoms of his desire, grief and solitude. The final sex scene is the most normative, and unsurprisingly is "real", following a chance encounter with a woman in Ballarat. This scene signals Gabor's growing control over the exotic, and his ability to use the exotica as a source of normative sex. The closing shot of the film is of the seashell, back in the landscape, waiting for another "victim". An oppressive choral soundtrack plays over the close up of the seashell, confirming it as the real cause of his deviation. The pornoexotic must show that even under extreme pressure (such as the hallucinogenic/shamanistic overtones of *Victoria Blue*), white heteronormativity remains the stable structure that transgressions reference, deviate from, and ultimately return to. The pornoexotic reinforces white heteronormativity precisely *because* of its unanalysed deviations that are ultimately satisfied within the limits of settler sexuality.

The outsider

The signification of Australia as an exotic location is highlighted by the naive experiences of an outsider. In *Lost in Paradise* and *Outback Assignment*, the second scene of the films is set in America, where the protagonists receive a phone call from Australia in which the country is described variously as 'in the middle of nowhere' and 'halfway around the world'. The reference to Australia's remoteness corresponds with the assumed exoticisation and eroticisation that such remoteness affords (Stratford and Langridge 2012). The decision to visit Australia has an element of coercion – a breakup, a mystery, a violent partner and a job offer too good to refuse. While their better judgement resists travelling to the exotic destination, circumstances compel them to make the journey. This is a necessary element of the exotic, whereby the traveller is excused of prurient interest by the urgency of their quest. Their lack of preparation leaves them open to the corruptive agency of the landscape which, as described in *Victoria Blue*, 'can play tricks on a man'.

A settler colony cannot be imagined as better than the metropole, neither is it a paradise that one associates with a holiday destination. Visitors who are also always potential citizens require careful advertising that offers an escape, a fresh start or a new opportunity in a system that is recognisable. In Australia, this is encapsulated by the common trope of the convict sent to the colony. Convict or not, the visitor is left with little option but to try and survive and ultimately thrive. All the pornoexotic films are a variation on this narrative that Australia is not a choice but a required destination.

What appears foreign and strange to the outsider is naturalised by the locals who look and sound uncannily familiar. This strange but familiar encounter is most apparent in *Lost in Paradise*. The premise of the film is that the protagonist, Donald Snow, was sent to Australia from America to shut down a lumber mill, but his subsequent disappearance sees the company send Jamie to investigate. Jamie disguises himself to infiltrate the community, only to find the mill still in operation. A one-minute shot with no dialogue shows the workings of an industrious mill. Jamie then learns that not only is the mill productive, but also that the community is polyamorous, valuing carnal and manual pleasures over profit. The production and consumption of a healthy, simple lifestyle is constantly referenced with characters playing tennis, going into town to an amusement park, going for walks across farms and attending bush dances.

Jamie represents the threat to this exotic paradise, and when unmasked is accused by Donald of coming to close down the mill. Donald refers to the mill as 'one of the few industries that keeps this town alive'. He goes on to describe his own transformation, claiming: 'I was making all this money to afford things I didn't want'. The company is presented as a hegemonic force threatening the alternative way of life. This "alternative" is merely a nostalgic longing for the stability of industrial capitalism. Particularly for American audiences, Australia represents a fiction of post-war harmonious domestic and work life. In *Lost in Paradise*, Jamie is convinced to stay and experience the community before making a decision as to its closure. The mill is ultimately saved by the discovery of a legal anomaly that invalidates the multinational corporation's claim. The son of the mill owner makes the discovery and decides to keep the mill in the family. Importantly the law is not broken and no independence is declared or defended with luck saving the community. Luck (the lucky settler and the lucky country

– as Australia is often referred to) is a word that is used to mask the violence (colonial, domestic, legal) that privileges the settler's body. Luck turns privilege into egalitarianism. Luck in a settler colony is genealogy, the process by which recognised relations inherit colonial spoils. The community Jamie encounters, and ultimately joins, is the perfect settler community. It is xenophobic, it is physically productive (providing the raw materials for construction), and it is owned and run by blood relations. Most importantly, sex and leisure are integrated into work. Sex is public, shared and displayed as a critical part of belonging to the community. White futurity in the *Lost in Paradise* community is the seamless combination of sex and work, both are enjoyable and a duty, both are protected and shared. The outsider meets the racial standard for the community, but it is not until he displays his loyalty through sharing sex, that he is admitted.

The exotic in *Lost in Paradise* is not of a "primitive" land radically different from and anathema to Western values. In fact, the exotic in all the films studied here assiduously avoids anything that could be recognised as radical difference. As Pease (2000, p. 129) states, 'the exotic is … shown to be a by-product of mass culture, a mass-produced, commodified fantasy perpetuated in culture through its representations'. It is the outsider and the audience that defines the Australian pornoexotic, which is constructed out of conservative, nostalgic fantasies of community and productivity promulgated by a global mass cultural memory. The outsider never encounters the Other but functions as a surrogate for the audience for whom 'in the context of post-modern sexual practice, the masturbatory voyeuristic technologically based fulfilment of desire is more exciting than actually possessing any real Other' (hooks 2006, p. 74). While the Other may be alluded to, it is simply a rhetorical device that strengthens the outsider's resolve to avoid difference and possession (being possessed by or being responsible for), preferring touristic voyeurism and unfettered access over analytical inquisitiveness. The outsider is as distanced as the audience; neither wants actual contact with an untranslated, unassimilated other. The difference with the outsiders in settler colonial porn is that their "return" to heteronormativity occurs within the exotic. The outsiders decide to remain because the community they find is heteronormative – put another way, it is "home-plus" (home plus sex). Once the outsider recognises the extra sex is not deviant, but a dutiful expression of settler sexuality, they are invited to settle.

Homosociality

The final characteristic of Australian pornoexotica is homosociality. The manner in which men have sex with other men in these films is heavily coded and linked to the broader notion of mateship that dominates discussions of masculinity in Australia. As Sedgwick (2015, p. 696) defines,

> concomitant changes in the structure of the continuum of male 'homosocial desire' were tightly, often causally bound up with the other more visible changes; that the emerging pattern of male friendship, mentorship, entitlement, rivalry, and hetero- and homosexuality was in an intimate and shifting relation to class; and that no element of that pattern can be understood outside of its relation to women and the gender system as a whole.

Sedgwick demonstrates the complex, and often contradictory yet overlapping relationship between homosexuality, homosociality and heterosexuality and their orbit in relation to real, imagined or absent women. The coding of sex between men as an expression of desire and a duty of mateship is necessarily made explicit in porn. Pornoexotica offers an insight into how sex between men is central to a settler colony and should not be seen as aberration, or as incidental, to nationalism. As we have seen, it is not the act in itself that is significant, but how it is understood and integrated – even, or particularly when it is considered "natural" – that determines what it means and does. For Australia, sex between men has to confront, or conform to, the demands of mateship. As such, the struggle for gay identity in a settler colony is always a political one as it struggles to seek validation outside of colonial hetero-masculine frameworks.

Mateship has been heavily critiqued, most obviously for its exclusion of women (Moreton-Robinson 2005). While gay men have been allowed into mateship, women are not as easily assimilated because of the centrality of misogyny to mateship. During the 1999 republic referendum in Australia, the idea of mateship became contentious as it was featured in the proposed preamble to the constitution. Although the preamble and the republic were separate issues, they were conflated in the public debate with mateship seen as part of a colonial identity that was being carried into a republic. The referendum and the preamble were defeated, and while mateship is not enshrined in the constitution it remains central to structuring Australian identity (as both a colony and independent nation).[8] Indeed, the very idea of enshrining mateship in the preamble attenuates mateship, as it operates best as unregulated networks of law, knowledge and power. For it to be part of the constitution it would open it up to "all citizens", and remove the exclusions it is built on. Further, mateship is dialectical, in that it is anti-establishment and patriotic, productive and lazy, egalitarian and exclusive, asexual and full of sex. Mateship holds small groups of men together in a similar fashion to the nuclear family, both have a role in the political organisation of the nation and both claim to be apolitical. This dichotomy of mateship is best captured by Ward's (1978, p. 1) definition of the Australian "legend",

> According to the myth the 'typical Australian' is a practical man, rough and ready in his manners and quick to decry any appearance of affectation in others. He is a great improviser, ever willing to 'have a go' at anything, but willing too to be content with a task done in a way that is 'near enough'. Though capable of great exertion in an emergency, he normally feels no impulse to work hard without good cause. He swears hard and consistently, gambles heavily and often, and drinks deeply on occasion. Though he is 'the world's best confidence man', he is usually taciturn rather than talkative, one who endures stoically rather than one who acts busily. He is a 'hard case', sceptical about the value of religion and of intellectual and cultural pursuits generally. He believes that Jack is not only as good as his master but, at least in principle, probably a good deal better, and so he is a great 'knocker' of eminent people unless, as in the case of his sporting heroes, they are distinguished by physical prowess. He is a fiercely independent person who hates officiousness and authority, especially when those qualities are embodied in military officers and policemen. Yet he is very hospitable and, above all, will stick to his mates through thick and thin, even if he thinks they may be in the wrong.

Ward is venerating mateship and masculinity here, and his book was very popular and influential in establishing the definition of the Australian male that is still referenced today. We can see in the first line that "Australian" and "man" are treated as one and the same. The rest of the definition involves a series of contradictions that equate to the work of colonisation. This myth of Australian identity is one that is formed around doing work as directed, but in a manner that looks like the work is not being done. In the Australian colonial narrative, white men doing the absurd work of settlement find solace and enjoyment in each other. Any public colonial relation outside of mateship is seen to be too directly implicated in the continued authority and expansion of the master who required the work in the first place. This is true of all settler colonies, but it is especially evident in Australia where forced convict labour was a large part of the expansion of early settlements. If the work is required but not believed in, then "authentic" relationships between men are generated through inauthentic work. Representations of mateship always revert to this position of the reluctant (but very competent) worker who finds joy in the performance of subversion that typically ends in greater than expected success (or symbolically significant sacrifice). In this way both the master and the worker get what they want and can proclaim success in spite of the other. The operation of mateship disguises white power hierarchies in Australia as egalitarianism, it also disguises the real profit and benefits of colonial labour that are afforded to male settlers. By always deferring to a higher, incompetent authority, the actual power that is accrued and shared between white men is effaced.

Mateship allows for almost any activity between white Australian men to be classified as between mates – this can particularly be observed in the co-opting of individual desire and sex into expressions of mateship. Mateship incorporates non-normative sex (group sex with more men than women) and sex between men as "non-sex". By non-sex I mean sex that is held separate to discourses of coupled heterosex (marriage, family, morality) and is desired and enjoyed based on this distinction. This enjoyment is not solely or even primarily sexual, it is discursive, ironic, denigrating, humorous and fictive. As Ward (2015, p. 4) argues, homosociality should be seen as a 'constitutive element' of heteronormativity. Further, that even if men having sex with men was critical of heterosexuality 'these practices typically … are not gay in their identitarian consequences, but are instead about building heterosexual men, strengthening hetero-masculine bonds, and strengthening the bonds of white manhood in particular'. Similarly Silva (2017) maintains that sex between straight men is "bud-sex" that reinforces heteronormative institutions. Mate-sex operates in the orbit of heterosex (rather than in opposition to it), while providing insulated opportunities for desire between men to be expressed without threatening hetero-relationships/identity.

The disparity between the number of men and women colonisers is the obvious reason for the centrality of homosociality in settler colonies. Settler colonies start with more men than women and this continues to be the case with immigration favouring men (selected for economic reasons, and hence the gender disparity in wage labour is replicated in migrant statistics making it easier for men to migrate to settler colonies). In the early settlement of Australia men outnumbered women three to one (Clark 1963, p. 77). The charter for the settlement of Australia recognised this problem and charged Governor Philip with picking up women along the first fleets' journey. Governor Philip ignored this directive, and the settlement started with 1,071 men and 265 women and children. The women were kept on a separate ship during the journey. This raises a contested moment in the settlement of Australia. While many nations mythologise being "founded in blood", Australia was founded in "orgy", an event that reportedly occurred on the 6 February, days after the first settlement ships arrived, and as a result of the women and children disembarking. The authenticity of the event has been questioned, Clark first popularising it in *A Short History of Australia* (1963, p. 25) but later doubted its actual occurrence. Only one primary written account remains from Arthur Bowes Smyth (1778), who stated,

> abt. 6 O'Clock p.m. we had the long wish'd for pleasure of seeing the last of them They were dress'd in general very clean & some few amongst them might be sd. to be well dress'd. The Men Convicts got to them very soon after they landed, & it is beyond my abilities to give a just discription of the Scene of Debauchery & Riot that ensued during the night.

Even this account has been contested as Smyth was not on shore that night (Karskens 2011), however the lack of evidence is not surprising as proof (defined by normative historical methods) of sexual violence is almost always absent. It would be reasonable to assume such an event happened (or versions of it, large and small). In fact, the evidence of mass rape and group sex is to be found in the increase in birth rate in the early settlement. Described as miraculous, with 'barren' women becoming pregnant, this fact remains largely unexamined, absurdly attributed to 'healthy living' and used as a signifier of the 'success' of the colony (Karskens 2009, pp. 323–5). Many letters back to England describe this occurrence, and it would be reasonable to assume that women who could not fall pregnant to their husbands, fell pregnant to other men. We know historically that women are typically blamed for infertility, whereas the reality is that infertility effects men in equal numbers. These letters home could not talk openly of rape, but in the coded language of 'miracles' we can find clues as to the sexual violence that is always part of colonial violence. Miraculous fertility was most probably caused by orgies, and these orgies would have been group rapes. The truth is that the settlement in Australia was founded by outnumbered women being "shared" amongst men – men who participated together in a ritual that tied mateship and group rape together, and above monogamous hetero-coupling. The myth of the singular 6 February orgy is most probably mythic not because it never occurred but because it was part of everyday life and not restricted to a lawless (literally before the declaration of colonial law) bacchanalian moment, as Hughes characterised (1987, p. 89).

As a myth the orgy has ongoing cultural significance, and hence it is important that it is often depicted as being encircled with redcoat soldiers. The soldiers had a dual function. The first was to keep the Indigenous Gadigal people from interfering or joining the orgy, and as such, is the first example of racial purity being policed in Australia. The other was to prevent women from escaping. It is revealing that the settler colony's first real act of sovereignty was the militarised protection of land, and the defining of land as property through the "labour" of mate-sex and rape. In the eyewitness account, the 'debauchery' occurred 'before they had all got their tents pitched or anything in order to receive them' (Smyth 1788). Sex came *before* the building of housing structures. If the central claim of this book is that sex is part of the colonial labour that justifies property claims over Indigenous peoples, then this account suggests sex is the *foundational* property claim in Australia. It was not permanent structures that defined the colonisers' claim, rather it was sex on land that prepared the ground for private property. In this light we can see the multiple scenes of sex in nature in pornoexotica to be property claims. Colonial futurity in Australia was enshrined in this founding complicity between military force, property rights and sex. This complicity continues today with various neocolonial measures that have expanded the reach and authenticity of white futurity. Pornography is part of such neocolonial measures by excluding Aboriginal people, showing white women as always willing subjects of male desire, showing sex in nature and depicting sex between men as homosocial and central to settler sexuality.

Most representations of mateship do not have to deal with the problem of sex between men directly. However, mateship in heteroporn encounters the same problem as the colonial pornoexotic. In presenting the fantasy combined with the necessity to "show it all" it may accidentally depict the reality of national homoerotica, displacing the required public relationship between settlement and monogamous heterosexuality. Heteroporn cannot use homoerotica as a latent background that deepens the bond between white men in the way that many other non-porn representations do because male desire must be explicitly satisfied in porn. Mateship is depicted in Australian pornoexotica and explicit sex is also depicted, but the combination assiduously avoids any validating, naming or recognising sex between men as an end in itself. Berlant and Warner (1998) define the difference between sexuality and pleasure, whereby sexuality has public accountability and pleasure deliberately avoids identification (or defaults to normative identity). Mate-sex in Australia seems to follow this and can be understood as a 'border intimacy [that] give people tremendous pleasure' (Berlant and Warner 1998, p. 561). However, it is difficult to describe it as a border intimacy as mateship and its validation through mate-sex, is so central to Australian identity. In fact, it may be more necessary to perform enjoyment in mate-sex because of the required "authentic" bonding outcome.

Mate-sex in Australian pornoexotica uses various tactics to avoid undermining itself. The main tactics are having women actively invite more men into the scene, placing sex scenes in public so they can be watched by other men, and intercutting sex scenes with mateship activities. The lack of consent and agency of women in a settler colony is distorted in pornography to suggest that the low number of women means they are always desiring male contact and thus consent is not an issue. Their enjoyment is assumed rather than assessed and sexual exclusivity is secondary to group sex opportunities. We could say all of these are common to heteroporn, but seen through the lens of colonial pornoexotica, these tactics do more than offer opportunities to expose women's bodies. These tactics connect sex to the narrative and setting, justifying sex between men in the logic of the filmic narrative and within broader representations of colonial mateship.

In *The Fugitive 2*, mateship and heterosexual coupling is deliberately contrasted. A foreign, jealous man chases his girlfriend across Australia because he cannot stand the idea of her having sex with other men. As she flees she encounters two local "mates" who protect her, eventually the jealous man is killed by a crocodile and the woman offers herself as a reward to the two men. The film ends with a group sex scene between the two men and the woman. In this instance the outsider is not accepted into the community because he places his partner over his proto-mates and refuses to share her. The woman, although always willing, is still described as a "reward" for the two men for protecting her. In another sex scene in the film, fantasy and reality are co-mixed when a man, sleeping next to other men in the bush has a sex dream, the dream is intercut with the man receiving a blow job while he sleeps. He eventually cums but does not wake up, nor do the other men sleeping around him. Here, the invisible woman who performs a sex act on the man does so while he sleeps with a group of men. Her invisibility to the other men in the scene folds her into a fantasy where she is the symbolic catalyst for sexual desire amongst the group. A similar fantasy/reality mate-sex scene occurs in *Pacific Blue*, where the hallucinogenic seashell makes his ex-girlfriend appear, who has sex with two men while he watches. At the conclusion of the scene she spits the other men's cum in his face. It is the colonial landscape that projects, against his will, the necessity for him to "share" his partner. In *Lost in Paradise*, an outdoor sex scene concludes by the camera panning across to reveal two previously unseen men who had been watching the action, applauding and saying "bravo" and "well done". The following scene features all three men drinking in a pub, discussing work, leisure and sex interchangeably. In these ways the non-sexual productive work of mateship produces the opportunities for sex. The men do not go looking for sex, but encounter it precisely because they are being good mates.

Conspicuous absence

The pornoexotic is a genre of white heteroporn that allows for the activation of exotic exception while maintaining the primacy of the desirability of white bodies. It shares similarities with other non-pornographic exotic representations but confronts the problem of having to close the fantasy through fucking. Instead of using this as an opportunity to give sexual agency and visibility to difference, it isolates the exotic as depoliticised signifiers and sexual catalyst. Settler colonial pornoexotica further complicates the exotic by being produced in a space that is also normative – it is both an advert and a warning, an exception and a project of nation building. Australian heteroporn demonstrates these complexities, and while there are national peculiarities in their deployment, variations of these complexities can be found in all European settler colonies. The films examined in this chapter do not depict any departure from iconic media representations of Australia, however, because the location is often shown to be an active element in the transgressions of the characters, it intrudes into the sex scenes causing unintentional ruptures. These are slight, but hint at the resistance of the environment to attempts to naturalise settler sexuality.

While the collapse of landscape and fucking (foreground and background) does offer opportunities for critique, the depictions of Blackness, in particular the Aboriginal people is more problematic. What is not seen in these films is just as important. The temptation with pornography is to be distracted by the explicit content, and analyse the sex as having primary significance. Like the audience, the academic often skips to the sex scenes and digs down into the sexual politics of various acts. However, what is not depicted and what is refused sexualisation holds a different significance. How these films avoid people of colour and references to Aboriginal desire while trading on the exotic requires careful and intentional structuring. It speaks to the broader issue of the absence of Indigenous people globally in pornography and the problematic micro-category of "Native" porn. There is seemingly an inability to incorporate Indigeneity into pornographic narratives. The following chapter will attempt to unpack this absent history and demonstrate the continued global impact of colonisation in censoring Indigenous desire, sexual agency and representation.

Notes

1 Wolfe argues that elimination is not necessarily the same as genocide. He states 'the settler-colonial logic of elimination has manifested as genocidal – they should be distinguished. Settler colonialism is inherently eliminatory but not invariably genocidal' (2006, p. 337). This means that elimination of Indigenous people can, in certain circumstances, be part of settler population growth through assimilation and miscegenation practices.
2 The legacy of the conflation of the exotic and erotic can be located in postcolonial and feminist critiques that describe non-pornographic representations of otherness as pornographic, using "the pornographic" as an analytical framework to denote exposure, exploitation and manipulation (Nash 2014, p. 7). While these critiques directly address ongoing colonisation of representation, particularly of Black women's bodies, the appeal to pornography in such a way does not reflect the complex and often contradictory effects of pornography.
3 *Pirates'* commercial success in 2006 needs to be contextualised by the rise in post-pornographic consumption. While the film was released before *Pornhub*, its success is not reflective of the broader shift towards free, non-feature porn. It may be the most successful, but it is not the most viewed. Despite this, its commercial success during a time of massive disruption in the porn industry is significant.
4 Production and distribution of pornography laws differ from state to state in Australia. There are also legislative differences between states and territories. The Australian Capital Territory is the most permissive of the states and territories in Australia regarding the production and distribution of pornography.

5 There are more contemporary pornographic films that are close to this category, such as Mr Nasty's *Aussie Fuckfest Canberra* (2007) and *Aussie Fuckfest Gold Coast* (2007) but these have minimal narrative and largely improvised dialogue, and represent the shift towards micro-budget, POV and gonzo pornography. Michelle Flynn's *Momentum Vol 1–4* (2015–2017) is part of a slow return to narrative films set in Australia. The Momentum series has won international recognition and is part of the ethical, authentic porn movement. Prior to this Anna Brownfield released *The Band* in 2008, and Ms Naughty released *The Fantasy Project* in 2014, both of these films are feature length, shot in Australia and part of an Australian feminist porn movement. I will be referring to some of these films in passing as they are related to but not exemplars of the Australian pornoexotic.

6 As Shimizu (2007, p. 108) notes in relation to early twentieth century heteroporn, 'the placement of excessive Orientalist signs indicates the importance of communicating the Other-ness of the locale and the people performing on screen so as to arouse pleasure in the stag film's male viewers'.

7 The beach has been a site of major racial conflict in Australia, including the Cronulla riots in 2005, the Manly Beach "rampage" on Australia Day in 2009 and white nationalist protests at St Kilda beach in 2019.

8 The first draft of the preamble included the phrase 'we value excellence as well as fairness, independence as dearly as mateship'. Following sustained criticism, then Prime Minister John Howard replaced the phrase with 'supportive of achievement as well as equality of opportunity for all'. In a press conference Howard expressed regret that he had been forced to remove the reference to mateship. See McKenna (2000) for an extensive history of the preamble.

2 The absence of Indigenous people in pornography

The invisibility of Indigenous people in heteroporn and the lack of scholarship around this absence is the focus of this chapter. I do not aim to speak for Indigenous people, nor try like so many white ethnographers before me, to explain, categorise, normalise, spectacularise or pathologise Indigenous desire and sex. Instead I am attempting to explain this absence historically as a symptom of the settler colonial representative structures that have, at various times, deployed pornographic strategies in representations of Indigenous people. The contemporary absence is in contrast to the hypervisualisation of ethnopornography in the late nineteenth and early twentieth century. I also do not wish to contribute to the invisibility by ignoring the radical potential of Indigenous pornographic resistance that currently exists. My focus on hegemonic patriarchal image systems, does not mean there is not important, vibrant work by Indigenous activists and artists that are producing alternate desires and pleasures.[1] To suggest total invisibility is to continue a settler's gaze that projects a passive attitude onto Indigenous people and to assume there is no agency, no pleasure, no desire that can act independently or critically of settler ideology. What I wish to address is the distribution and censorship of heteroporn and lay out the mechanisms that prevent settler's fantasies of Indigenous people from being represented. In particular, I am interested in the way Indigenous sex has been separated from ritual by colonial law, ethnography and politics, such that attempts to preserve and protect Indigenous culture deliberately excludes sexual practices. The questions I ask are: Why is Indigenous sex and desire not co-opted, exploited or misread into racial pornographic fantasies consumed by settlers? Why aren't settlers producing pornographic "Native" narratives that intensify race and desire and allow the possibility of Indigenous identification and critique within dominant cultural modes?

Porn studies in settler colonies has advanced to the point that texts offering a Butlerian (2013) "aggressive counter-reading" of porn, exemplified by Nash's *Black Body in Ecstasy* (2014), offer radical and strategic pathways through racist pornography.[2] Nash argues that the hyper-performance of race in these films combined with the obvious performativity of the genre means that it is immanently open to critique in its viewing. This critique continues into the "real" fucking, such that desires, inversions and pleasures are complicated even while seeming to enforce stereotypes. The complexity of racialised porn opens up possibilities for different types of spectatorships, witnessing and pleasure for the actors and the audience. Black audiences can find moments of ecstasy in racist pornography that are both complicated and compelling. Such analysis contests the assumption of porn's history as one that is only capable of erasing Black agency. These re-readings are vital in expanding porn studies, and its intersection with Black feminism. Porn studies has predominantly been advanced in settler colonies, with subtle, radical and political potential uncovered in its representations of race located in even the most heteronormative examples. Against this backdrop the invisibility of Indigenous people, of a differently racialised body, is doubly concerning. First, the issue of representation has to be addressed before re-representational strategies are available. Second, the issue of representation is posed from within a dominant system that is already perforated with re-representational creative and critical frameworks that have thus far excluded Indigenous people. The absence of Indigenous people in porn is a settler colonial elimination strategy that speaks to a fear of a radical alterity of Indigenous futurity that colonisation itself created and now censors.

Ethnopornography

Pornographic representations have not always excluded Indigenous people. From the nineteenth century to the early twentieth century ethnopornography of Indigenous people was common and popular across settler colonies. It was an early form of pornoexotica, using the rubric of anthropology to be distributed into male personal libraries under the pretext of education.[3] The current absence of Indigenous people in pornography should be read against their previous hypervisualisation. As Nash (2014, pp. 5–6) argues,

> Racial iconography shows that the history of racialized pornography contains moments where black female bodies have been

'overexposed,' and other moments when black women have been wholly absent from hard-core pornography. In challenging the hegemonic overexposure account, racial iconography asks new and historically specific questions, including how do we interpret black women's absences from the pornographic visual field in particular historical moments? How can we read those absences against pornography's strategic mobilization of black women's bodies in other social, historical, cultural, and technological moments?

Elizabeth Povinelli's (2002, p. 82) account of ethnopornography by nineteenth century anthropologists such as Lorimer Fison, Baldwin Spencer and Francis Gillen evidences how their work directly influenced the structuralism of anthropologists from Lewis Morgan to Alfred Radcliffe-Brown to Lévi-Strauss who sought to 'formalize these elaborate [ethnoporn] corporeal intercourses into multiple models of heterosexually regimented familial organization'. While ethnopornography has been largely erased from the history of anthropology, its impact on normative definitions and justifications of white heteronormativity was clear throughout the twentieth century. Further, as Balce (2006, pp. 96–7) argues, ethnopornography's influence spread beyond the academy into early pornographic distribution networks of postcards and journals such as *National Geographic* 'which functioned as a "wellspring of masturbatory fantasies" for a generation of fin de siècle American men'.

Pornography's indexical claim is born both of its medium and its historic link to ethnography, as Hansen *et al.* (1991, p. 210) argue 'pornography is a strange, "unnatural" form of ethnography, salvaging orgasmic bliss from the seclusion of the bedroom'. Ethnopornography provided a "truth" about Indigenous people, in the Foucauldian tradition of "sex speak". It told a truth of 'naked, howling savages who have no idea of permanent abodes, no clothing ... [whose sex was] crude in the extreme' (Spencer and Gillen 1904, p. xiv). Ethnopornography's "truth" of Indigenous sex was signified by the casual presence of nudity, defined by Western categories of clothed and naked, such that 'female nudity [was used] to justify imperial violence and articulate colonial phantasms about the savage land' (Balce 2006, p. 90). These fashion cues map onto binaries of nature and culture that underpin colonial Native/non-Native racial hierarchies. Any visual ethnography of Indigenous people was pornographic due to its depiction of nudity as inseparable from Indigeneity. Further, as the anthropologists Spencer and Gillen reported, nudity and 'crude' sex were indicators of 'no permanent abode' and hence became woven into sovereignty arguments. A person who is naked in public must not have a "home" – private property being the only place for nudity.

These narratives and images are precisely what we would expect to find, although it is important to note that the anthropologists who produced this pornography often framed it against the looming shadow of colonisation. They were recording fragments of rituals, or performances of rituals that were done for the benefit of the anthropologist because these rituals were seen as passing into history. As Wolfe (1999) and Clark (2016) argue this means that Indigeneity is imagined as always already dying. As Rosaldo (1989, p. 108) states 'imperialist nostalgia revolves around a paradox: A person kills somebody, and then morns the victim'. Ethnopornography is part of the salacious morning of Indigenous sex, it was a celebration of the victory of colonisation in its masturbatory mourning. The othering justified colonisation, not only on moral grounds but as incompatible: it was not that Indigenous sex was animalistic, but that it had a structure and narrative which could be pruriently recorded for colonial consumption while remaining totally incompatible with modern sexuality. Such fictional narratives were easily incorporated into colonial representational systems, and 'circulated through a textual field saturated with fictional and nonfictional accounts of savage lives and times' (Povinelli 2002, p. 79). This circulation slowed and all but ended by the mid twentieth century, with very few new images entering ethnopornography. During this time the highly sexualised, fetishised Indigenous body disappears from colonial representational systems. Of course, this erasure did not mark the end of rape or miscegenation as colonial weapons, there was something specific to settler colonisation that made such sexual fantasies anathema to developing colonial structures. I argue there are two reasons for this, the first is that as settler colonies began to see themselves as nations, they could not sustain an alterity inside their own borders, and second elimination strategies of settler colonies prevented Indigenous sexual agency from being represented for fear it indicated a desire for Indigenous futures outside of miscegenation.

As settler colonies claimed various levels of symbolic and legal independence, control shifted from internal frontiers to external threats. As Povinelli (2002, p. 77) asks, 'did the lack of a common language or shared moral universe between settler and indigenous groups threaten the very notion of an Australian nation before there was a nation in fact?' The very thing ethnopornography traded on becomes a threat to a newly founded nation state's obsession with appearing whole and intact. Povinelli (2002, p. 112) articulates the problem of granting Indigenous people citizenship,

> How could a modern, civil nation condone a state-sanctioned space of sexual immorality, perversion, and violence? How could the indigenous population be integrated into the nation and be given equal citizenship rights and responsibilities while they maintained customs antithetical to civil society? And how could the state enforce a policy that so clearly violated the common-sense limit of human right and decency?

Ethnopornography and anthropology become defined along moral lines. Anthropology's role was to separate ritual from sex, so that one could be preserved as culture, and the other erased as incompatible with colonial citizenship. The limit that Povinelli refers to is a sexual one, argued on moral grounds. The effect was the emergence of a different discourse on Indigenous sex, not one of radical alterity and fascination, but of problems and perversions within structures of modern sexuality. Indigenous sex is something to be policed, regulated, criminalised rather than masturbatorially mourned. This shift will be examined through *The Northern Territory National Emergency Response* ('The Intervention') in Australia, which banned pornography in Indigenous communities and was instigated because of false claims of rampant child sex abuse in Aboriginal communities. More broadly this shift is an attempt to separate culture and sex, which takes culture as something that is preserved and "museumified" and sex as unpredictable, dangerous and future orientated. This separation underlines a change in settler strategies to regulate, and ultimately erase Indigeneity. This distinction, and erasure, can even be found in Indigenous victories, such as the Australian High Court decision in *Mabo and Others v. Queensland (No. 2)*. *Mabo* is seen by the progressive settler public as a victory for Aboriginal land rights. However, the ruling contains the following as a limit on customary law and culture; they are permitted 'provided those laws and customs are not so repugnant to natural justice, equity and good conscience' (Mabo 1992, HCA 23).[4] The fear in this quote reflects the legacy of ethnopornography – a legacy that has been normalised through anthropology's separation of sex and culture, and is actively policed through the requirements of settler citizenship. By appealing to some sort of universal standard, it marks Indigenous people as positioned (or desiring to return) outside of universal morality which itself is a position invented by colonisation's requirement to make categories of Native, slave and settler incompatible. Ultimately such conditions underline neocolonial elimination strategies masked as decolonial gestures.

It is important to note that the *United Nation's Declaration on the Rights of Indigenous People*, adopted in 2007, makes no mention of sex, sexuality or bio-reproductive rights. The same separation of culture from sex exists in the charter,

> *Recognizing* the urgent need to respect and promote the inherent rights of indigenous peoples which derive from their political, economic and social structures and from their cultures, spiritual traditions, histories and philosophies, especially their rights to their lands, territories and resources.
> (United Nations General Assembly 2007, p. 3)

The document defends the authenticity of everything except Indigenous sex and sexualities in an omission which, intentional or not, reproduces a colonial definition of Indigeneity as devoid of sexual agency or rights independent of those defined by nation states and supranational institutions. By not being able to speak of sex directly this declaration of Indigenous rights turns into metaphor precisely at the point it defends Indigenous futurity,

> Indigenous peoples have the right to practise and revitalize their cultural traditions and customs. This includes the right to maintain, protect and develop the past, present and future manifestations of their cultures, such as archaeological and historical sites, artefacts, designs, ceremonies, technologies and visual and performing arts and literature.
> (United Nations General Assembly 2007, p. 11)

In avoiding directly naming sex, 'metaphor invades decolonization, it kills the very possibility of decolonization; it recenters whiteness, it resettles theory, it extends innocence to the settler, it entertains a settler future' (Tuck and Yang 2012, p. 2). Typically, where official discourse avoids direct references to sex, pornography fills the gap, but that has not happened for Indigenous people, caught in an official metaphor that separates desiring bodies from land and culture. Without naming Indigenous sex, all that can be imagined in porn and the United Nations declaration is limited by settler futurity.

Black porn/elimination strategies

Black studies and Black feminisms have provided substantial historical and theoretical accounts for Black men and women in pornography. However, these frameworks do not explain the absence of Indigenous people in pornography. This is largely because of pornography's own particular definition of Blackness which is restricted to African American people. Interracial as a dominant porn category is defined as white (Americans) and African Americans, and typically between white women and Black men. As Landes and Nielsen's (2018, p. 118) study into 10,000 porn performers found, actors who refused interracial scenes (47 per cent of white female porn actors) were really refusing African American men, as 'Asian or Latino performers do not seem so much affected by racial dodging'. Heteroporn's own racialisation of Blackness has directed most of the critique, which unsurprisingly traces the racial dynamic to slavery. Seen as evidence of sexual excess, hyper-fecundity and alterity, interracial porn amplifies stereotypes specific to histories of race that are inextricably linked to slavery. Counter critiques which salvage ecstasy, racialised excitement and deconstructions of race in their hyper-performance, still take slavery in America as the instigator of racialised narratives in pornography. Read as either sexual violence against Black bodies, or as a starting point for destabilising the same violence, Blackness in pornography is a symptom of one aspect of settler colonial violence. Indigenous Blackness has been erased in pornography, yet interracial porn remains (with some fluctuations) hypervisual across modern and contemporary pornography. This difference can be mapped to the different ideological framing of Native and slave by settler colonies. Wolfe (1999, p. 2) writes of the 'hyperfecundity, natural sense of rhythm, etc. that are typically attributed to slave races', and it is this discourse which is translated into interracial porn. Because the profit of slave owners was linked to both the labour of the slave and their reproduction, narratives of excess (strength, virility, fertility etc.) were common. The same narrative was not applied to Indigenous people, even though their labour and sex was forced and profited from by colonists. The ideology of elimination is a type of settler violence that is contrapuntal to the ideology of hyperfecundity that marks slavery.

The colonial distinction between Native and non-Native is not a racial determination but primarily an economic one. This economic distinction, in turn, rests on a Lockean definition of labour that excludes Indigenous sovereignty on the basis of economics (as explored further in Chapter 3). As Wolf (1999, p. 2) argues, 'in the settler-colonial economy, it is not the colonist but the native who is superfluous'. Necessarily superfluous in an ideological sense that justified settlement rather than reflecting the lived reality of colonised people. Native was generated as a remainder category, 'thus "non-Native" signifies not a racial or ethnic identity but a location within settler colonialism' (Morgensen 2011, p. 3). All non-Natives are stratified into locations within settlement, whose locations are racialised after the primary Native/non-Native separation. Non-Natives operate economically within settler colonies (to be exploited or to exploit), and these positions change over time, accruing and losing value. These fluctuations are witnessed in the distribution of the sensible, that has historically mapped and produced the shifting value of differently racialised people. This value which treats the Black subject as a literal commodity, is contextualised and critiqued in Black feminism's account of racialised people in pornography. "Black" as a racialised category within non-Native has always had an economic value, and hence has always been distributed into the sensible dragging with it histories of exploitation, challenges and ruptures of the sensible that are entangled in contemporary porn's representation of Blackness. This value has been directly calculated by Landes and Nielsen (2018) who found that white porn actors may be refusing African American men because the amount they are paid after performing interracial porn is reduced.[5] However the Native/non-Native distinction precedes this type of racialisation, and relies on different colonial histories that strip value, and its associated erotic imagination, from Indigenous people. As Tuck and Yang (2012, p. 12) notes,

> Through the one-drop rule, blackness in settler colonial contexts is expansive, ensuring that a slave/criminal status will be inherited by an expanding number of 'black' descendants. Yet, Indigenous peoples have been racialized in a profoundly different way. Native Americanness is subtractive: Native Americans are constructed to become fewer in number and less Native, but never exactly white, over time.

The subtractive/additive, replacement/exploitative, Native/non-Native distinction as defined by Tuck and Yang, Moreton-Robinson, Morgensen and Wolfe describes the ideology of elimination that structures colonial violence towards Indigenous peoples. Native as a left-over category, as something that is subtracted by the contact of colonisation, means that Native ultimately becomes an empty category, in which finally no person is authentically Native. The authentic Native becomes that of a culture removed from desiring bodies and preserved within colonial structures. Once Native is abstracted from the body, porn has nothing to represent, exploit or stereotype. Further, if Indigenous people were represented in porn, the subtractive rule means that such a representation would be a dutiful demonstration of making white, rather than an additive fear/attraction of Blackness as in interracial porn. Ethnopornography was the last moment in which both making white and fear/attraction could be exploited. Once the vanguard of ethnographers touched the "Native" its pornographic value evaporated. Indigenous "interracial" porn dissolves itself – porn is a medium of colonial touching, where the medium and distribution of representation makes all who are represented in it non-Native.

Settler sexuality

Settler sexuality and modern sexuality can be thought together as products of contact with Indigenous sex and futurity. Stoler's (2010) account of settler sexuality inverts the directional development of modern sexuality to claim that it was not imported to the colonies but was first developed there due to the specific conditions of settlement. Morgensen (2011) develops this argument to suggest that Indigenous sexuality was the original queering that became the departure point for modern sexuality. This queering was a crucial organising structure of invasion and settlement, as Morgensen (2011, p. xii) maintains, ' "settler sexuality" queers Native peoples to attempt their elimination compatibly with emphasizing racialized heteropatriarchal control over subject people of color placed on Native lands'. The queering of Indigenous people cast them outside of modern sexuality as part of a primitive narrative in a necessary move to make Indigenous sovereignty and futurity incompatible with modern civilisation.

The invention of modern sexuality occurs through the settlement process that sought to vanquish "primitive" sexuality. This process occurred both within the settler, as a control of desire towards hetero-colonial goals, and through the elimination of Indigenous people and their futures. The former is the focus of most heteronormative critique, including Foucault for whom colonisation was outside his analytic concern (Stoler 1995). The separation of sexuality from colonisation abstracts "primitive" to psychoanalytic, evolutionary or European traditions, theories and histories that haunt white subjects. It also abstracts colonisation to be a radial condition of modern (European) life, rather than seeing it as its material defining factor. The radical alterity of Indigenous sex and sexuality is that it is defined as *without awareness of modern sexuality*. This colonial definition denies Indigenous sexuality, genders and practices a position within modern sexuality. Anyone brought into colonial structures (including Indigenous people) are necessarily made aware of modern sexuality and are therefore no longer capable of Indigenous sex. For Indigenous people this manifests in miscegenation, colonial sexual violence and the pathologising of sex according to settler morality. However, the notion of a radical alterity of Indigenous sex remains silently at the centre of modern sexuality, despite its assumed elimination by the total reach of global neocolonisation. The regulation of sexuality, both internally by the settler and as a process of colonisation work together to reinforce modern sexuality's connection to settlement. As Stoler (2010, p. 78) articulates 'sexual control was both an instrumental image for the body politics – a salient part standing for the whole – and itself fundamental to how racial policies were secured and how colonial projects were carried out'.

A further consequence of queering all Indigenous sex as not located in specific acts, but as a defining characteristic of Indigeneity, is that it encourages and excuses savage settler sexuality. Povinelli (2002, p. 146) states,

> Settler sexuality and settler immorality erased the clean line between the 'horrible rites' of native society and the quotidian practices of settler society. Settlers did not just think, look, imagine, and feel implicated in indigenous sex acts as critical judges, but they did this also as critical actors: they knew it, they were the condition of it, they did no differently.

If modern sexuality was first played out on the frontiers of settler colonies, then modern sexuality is the making savage of settlers' own sexual violence. It is not violence in an abstract or internalised sense, as understood through its distribution to Europe, but the real violence of the colonist against the soon to be, or already, colonised. This suggests that heteronormativity emerges from a frontier history that defined itself against a savagery it inflicted and then projected onto its victims. This seeming paradox is the silencing of sexual violence that founded modern sexuality. Settler sexual violence is not a perversion or translation of European norms, but the material of them, mined in the colonies to be fabricated, reconstituted and distributed to the metropoles.

Native (American) porn

Pornography as a representational distribution system for modern sexuality can be thought of as primarily racially categorised. 'All porn is in essence race play porn, whether it overtly highlights racial contrasts or elides them by erasing racial difference from its representations', argue Smith and Luykx (2017, p. 434). Similarly, Shimizu (2007, p. 140) states that 'porn shelves are organized by race'. A racialised categorisation of porn is obvious on large aggregate porn sites as a hierarchising of different bodies' erotic value. In this sense, race is central to understanding the organisation and distribution of all pornography, and it has developed a clear structure around terms such as Black, Ebony, Asian, Latin, Eastern European and so on. These racialised terms were developed alongside and within modern sexuality as signifiers of value to white heteropatriarchy. Pornography's explicit content and racial categorisation appears to be totalising. Even the question as to which bodies are absent seems to go against the very definition of porn as a documentary and exploitative form. Access to, and the viewership of porn exemplifies the feeling of dominance associated with total visibility. 'The world of total visibility', Rancière (1999, p. 104) tells us, 'carves out a real where appearance has no place to occur or to produce its divisive, fragmenting effects'. The totalising visibility of porn censors the appearance of that which is assumed to have already been accounted for – in this case Indigenous people. The "complete" structure of pornography naturalises settler sexuality. As such Indigenous appearance in pornography, on the rare occasions when it occurs, either slips into ambiguous zones that occludes even mis-categorisation or is appropriated into settler roleplay. In the former, fragmentation and division are avoided through the vague and confused use of the term "Native".

"Native" is a remainder term used on sites such as *YouPorn* and *Pornhub* to designate an otherness that resists racial eroticisation. As Whitten and Corr (2001) note, there are very few terms to distinguish Native people. Native, Aboriginal, Indigenous are colonial terms that flatten the differences between First Nations and deny sovereignty. When such terms are used in porn they carry this confusion towards a body that appears ready to be racially labelled, but for whom no such label can be found. It can apply to porn made in Africa, or South America, ethnopornography, or Native Americans, but in each case it indicates a confused relationship to its own display. "Native" is used to term a curiosity or oddity rather than an erotic value. This can be evidenced first in the minuscule number of examples of "Native", with 1,208 results on *Pornhub* (which is 0.00012 per cent of total videos) and "Indigenous" which has only 14 results. Interestingly, on *YouPorn* there are 159 results for "Native" and the exact same number, and same videos for "Indigenous" which suggest they have been dual tagged. General observations of the videos tagged "Native" indicates a confusion, with a wide variety of people who have, for opaque reasons, fallen into this category. Within this micro-category "Native American" is the most common term, ascribing a geographic location for bodies determined by uploaders to be Native. This is to be expected with the majority of content on large aggregate sites being produced in America.

I will make some observations of the 1,208 videos that are tagged "Native" on *Pornhub*. These observations are problematic and can only provide a sketch of the dynamic across the videos. This analysis is a starting point to offer a global context for my discussion of the absence of Indigenous Australian pornography. The ambiguity in my analyses is primarily because in only one of the videos does the actor verbally identify as Indigenous (*Teens Loves huge Cocks – Tight Lipped*). My analysis uses the titles of the videos themselves, not as proof of Indigeneity, but as an indication that the uploader wanted the content to be racialised as Native. Of the 1,208 videos, 765 had "Native" in the title, the rest had no indication of why they had been tagged "Native" other than appearing to feature non-white people. Title analysis can suggest how "Native" is used within a system that excludes it. The first observation is precisely the problem of such observations, namely that Indigenous actors are identified by non-Native others. A lack of language around Indigeneity, or explicit racial play in the videos suggests there are limited scripts for eroticising Native sex play, even when the videos are explicitly named as Native. The vast majority of the videos display explicit heterosex and do not appear to differ from non-Native heteroporn. Perhaps most striking is that in almost all cases Native refers to the woman. This judgement is made through the titles which always indicated one "Native", and either did not mention the male's ethnicity, *Native girlfriend giving good morning head* or racialised the man as non-Native, *Native American girl fucks black bf*, *Native and White Guy Reverse Cowboy*. This is an inversion of typical interracial porn, and combined with heteroporn tropes, suggest the operation of the "one-drop" rule, where this porn is a demonstration of making white (or Black). Such interracial inversions are common in other racialised categories, however the almost complete absence of Native couples in the 1,208 videos is significant. The logic of elimination can be found in both the small number of examples of "Native" porn and that Indigenous futurity (porn with only Native actors in the title) has only been uploaded by two users, both of whom identify as Indigenous. Despite being a confused, remainder category in porn, it has a very clear, absolute limit – that that non-Natives have no contact with Native only porn.

Most of the videos are amateur, which is not surprising considering the nature of heteroporn on *Pornhub*. However, there are some professional videos on the site, which raises the issue of Native American pornstars. From my research I would suggest there are between 20 to 40 Native American pornstars who are currently working, or have worked, in the porn industry. Almost all are contemporary, with only Hyapatia Lee having worked in the industry in the 1980s. The existence of Native American pornstars suggests that the elimination narrative and incompatibility with modern sexuality argument is not accurate. However how these actors are framed, and frame themselves reveals the complexities of Native American porn identity. First, the ambiguity in the number is because many of the actors have not publicly self-identified as Indigenous. Their involvement in porn is as actors of colour, rather than as Native American pornstars (with the exception of Zaya Cassidy). Of the actors indexed on *Babepedia* all have a list of different ethnicities, even Zaya Cassidy who identifies as 100 per cent Cherokee is listed as 'mixed-race (primarily Caucasian)'. Others such as Ricky White are listed with an ethnicity of Caucasian, but the notes state 'Irish, Italian, and Native American descent'.[6] Out of the professional Native videos on *Pornhub*, only two have narratives that have Native American characters: *A Native story of Jennifer Jacobs (Before-After)* and *Big Tit Pornstars dressed up as Native Americans suck pilgrims big cocks*. Both of these films are set in the nineteenth century with non-Native actors playing Native roles. These two videos are the remnants of ethnopornography where first contact has been turned into white roleplay. Just how important the tension between before and after contact, or the pre-porn and post-porn body, is seen in *A Native story of Jennifer Jacobs (Before-After)*. The before and after in the title refers to before and after colonial contact, which in this case is colonial sex. A picture in picture shows a "Native American" before contact, while the central picture depicts the fucking between a white man and the "Native American". The fact that both images are shown simultaneously demonstrates an awkward attempt to invest the image with erotic fiction. The Native before contact has no value for pornography and hence cannot be shown by itself, yet the fucking in itself has no fantastical eroticism because it destroys the fantasy of a savage yet ignorant sexuality. The display is caught between these two images, requiring both, but ultimately failing to find an erotic language *between* these images.

Most Native American porn actors are seen by the industry as mixed race. On the *Internet Adult Film Database* there are only four films that star Native Americans playing Native American characters: Hyapatia Lee in *Native Tongue* (1993); Lezley Zen, in *Native American Ass* (2007); Zaya Cassidy in *I Neva Let A Hoe Go* (2016); and *Zaya Cassidy is Poke-Ahontas* (2017).[7] Lezley Zen and Zaya Cassidy have also played Latin roles: *Latin Extreme 2* (2002); and *Juicy Latin Pussy 3* (2017). Even when these actors are discussed for their Indigenous status the elimination narrative is explicit. Kingwin's (2018) article *Top 20: Native American Pornstars* exemplifies the elimination narrative,

> **Please be aware:** Native Americans are almost extinct so while these pornstars won't all be 100% Native American, we did find a lot of girls in porn business that have a gene or two of original American Indians.

Kingwin (2018) lists the variety of ethnicities under each actor, and a number of times questions the authenticity of their Indigeneity: 'Some of them could be lying but we can't check their DNA to find out the truth. These are self-proclaimed pornstars with Native American genes'. He also discusses the problem of audiences finding these actors, hinting at the lack of specific search terms, 'On a side-note, is anyone else bugged by the "Indian" name? Just makes things harder to find'. Kingwin's article falls into the romance of elimination narrative, stating, 'the saddest part is that there are just very few remaining women that can honestly claim this rare ethnicity'. Yet on the other hand he eroticises mixed ethnicity, 'Bella Bellz is part Italian, Asian and part Native American. Has inherited the best qualities for every gene pool'. Despite stating all on his list have self-identified as Native American, I have not been able to verify his claim. As the only listicle on Native American porn actors, it is significant that it reinforces both the elimination narrative and the one-drop rule, obsessively referencing and questioning ethnicity. While it attempts to eroticise specific characteristics of Native Americans and pines for authenticity, it is confused as to porn's role as both part of the elimination and its potential to eroticise authenticity. A counter-reading could argue that this article is a step forward, in that at least it exists, and it attempts, confusedly, to discuss the potential erotic value of Native Americans.[8] There are a few small moments of visibility, but these have not yet even established pornographic stereotypes as a space for identification and critique. Further it is not true that development of a settler stereotype is required *before* critical Indigenous representational autonomy can be achieved.

There are two videos from the collection of 1,208 videos tagged as "Native" on *Pornhub* that I wish to focus on, as they encapsulate the two separate problems porn has in dealing with Indigenous people. The first is an amateur video, the content of which is typical of heteroporn: it is a single scene featuring a blowjob and fucking. However, the title is a meta-title for Native porn: *100% Navajo 0% Pornstar*. This identification suggests a sliding scale, that the more Native a person is the less of a pornstar they can be. It aligns to the separation of Native from settler sexuality, in which Native is classified as ignorant of modern sexuality. The impossibility of an "authentic" Native person to also be a pornstar marks the success of colonial strategies to strip futurity, agency and desire from Indigenous people, and mark Indigenous sex as incompatible with not only settler futures, but the representation of that future making. *0% Pornstar* is the impossibility for representations of Native sex to exist within pornography and have any distributive value. The video is a statement of potential future value (the becoming settler of the Native), rather than a claim of erotic distributive value in itself.

The second video, which is actually two videos both titled *Little Native American Girl Fucking a Horse Cock* is of a solo masturbating woman dressed in a stereotypical Native American costume who identifies her ethnicity on her profile as Latin. In these videos we have a demonstration of what Tuck and Yang (2012) discuss as the handing over of Indigeneity to the coloniser for safe-keeping. In this 'move to innocence' the settler insists on the looming elimination by adopting and appropriating Native culture (Mawhinney 1999).[9] In porn there is a second step, it separates Native culture, essentially desexualising it, only to then re-sexualise it through the settler's body. The non-Native woman masturbating in "Native" costume is reconnecting sex and culture, but as appropriated within the settler and settler culture. Once dislocated from elimination narratives, the "Native" can be eroticised as settler roleplay. As Morgensen (2011, p. 52) understands such roleplays as 'citing native sexual pasts to inspire in non-natives a sexual future'. This video is an echoed fantasy of ethnopornography, safely inhabited by non-Native bodies for a non-Native audience. In this ethno-performative space, the "savagery" of Native sex is folded into visual settler sexual culture. The savagery is signified in the costume and in the horse dildo the actor uses. It is not a co-incidental paring, the "savage" replaced by a non-Native person and the "savage act" replaced by a silicon sex toy. What would be incompatible and illegal settler sex acts are sanitised into allowable taboos through the audio visual, synthetic industry of sex toys and webcams.

Two key issues prevent the appearance of Native porn by, and for, Indigenous people: first the normalisation of settlers playing Native roles and second the routine questioning of porn actors' self-identification, and insistence on multi-ethnic labelling. These two issues are products of the history outlined in this chapter and are part of broader settler sexual culture which, as Morgensen (2011, p. 1) states 'vanquish[es] sexual primitivity, which white settlers nevertheless adopt as their own history'. Multi-ethnic labelling in Native porn is part of the bureaucratically recorded process of making white (but never becoming white) and settler's playing "Native" is what Deloria (1998) identifies as the desire for settlers to become Indigenous through 'playing Indian'. The debates that have fuelled porn studies' examination of Blackness in porn and offered multiple pathways for critical analysis and porn production have not been brought to bear on the Native/non-Native racialisation. Despite Native being a micro-category that is almost invisible, it is critical in understanding all subsequent racialisations that occur across non-Native porn. The condition of being both invisible and yet structuring all porn reproduces the relationship between the settler state and Indigenous sovereignty more broadly. Settler sovereignty is ontologically anti-Indigenous yet paradoxically it is structured by Indigeneity. Pornography, as the representational technology of settler sexuality is formed and maintained by the same paradox. I have sketched this Native/non-Native representative binary as the basis to discuss the representation of Indigenous Australians in porn and demonstrate how specific recent histories of official settler violence have directly contributed to the current total absence of Aboriginal pornstars.

"Aboriginal" porn

There are currently no porn actors who publicly identify or are identified in marketing as Aboriginal, and 'almost no history of sexualized Aboriginality in the Australian genre' (King 2005, p. 533).[10] On large international porn databases such as *Pornhub* and *YouPorn*, "Aboriginal" is used as a term for generic Black otherness and

Indigeneity that is not specific to Australia. Even when used in this broader sense it yields only 36 and three results on *Pornhub* and *YouPorn* respectively. The 36 "Aboriginal" results on *Pornhub* follow a similar pattern to the results for "Native": 17 have "Aboriginal" in the title, 14 of those relate to a woman, two refer to a man (*Aussie … aboriginal dick from sydney*, *Bitch sucking some aboriginal dick*) and one is ambiguous as to gender (*Aboriginal porn*). None of the videos are professional, none have a narrative or plot. None of the actors verbally identify as Indigenous, and only one uploader identifies as Aboriginal.

In the four Australian feature heteroporn films studied in Chapter 1, the absence of Aboriginal people is on first examination unusual, as one would expect that the pornoexotic's primary signifier of the exotic would be the use of racial cues. Despite this, there is a stark absence of Aboriginal people in Australian heteroporn, except for one scene in *Outback Assignment* (1991). From the cover of the DVD, it is implied that the Aboriginal character plays a dominant role in this film. She is the only figure on the cover and is adorned in generic "primitive" costume (a leopard-print top, leather loin cloth and braided hair band). Despite her centrality on the DVD cover she plays a minor role in the film, appearing only in the first sex scene where she does not speak, and is not referred to by name. The actor is credited as Nioka and has appeared in three other films set in Australia, however, it is only in *Outback Assignment* that she plays an Aboriginal character. Andrew King (2005, p. 524) refers to her character as one of the many instances of the 'use [of] non-Aboriginal actors in the roles of indigenous characters (adorned with body paint)'.

This scene opens with Tucker alone in the bush, boiling tea over a fire. This references the iconic image of the solitary white man in the Australian bush boiling a "billy" (a pot used to boil water for tea), which can be found in paintings such as Frederick McCubbin's *Down on his Luck* (1889). Nioka walks out of the bush alone. She wears only a loincloth and what appears to be a bone necklace and earrings. She is carrying a shield and walks towards Tucker. The viewer is presented with contradictory symbols of fashion, nature, sound and narrative. Geczy (2014) argues a difference between being out of fashion and being outside fashion. The latter is reserved for the pre-modern, as their fashion does not function in the Barthian (1983) sense but rather as someone who is an uninitiated subject of fashion's gaze. The paradox for Nioka is that she can be clearly located *in fashion*, as her costume, hair and makeup place her in the late 1980s, but she plays a character who has had no contact with fashion. Similar to *A Native story of Jennifer Jacobs (Before-After)* her costume signifies her as both before and after settler contact.

At first Tucker does not notice her, and it is not her physical presence that captures his attention but the sound of a didgeridoo. The sound startles him and he looks down at his tea, suggesting that he may have unintentionally drunk something that was hallucinogenic. The otherworldliness of the Native is depicted as incompatible with the conscious, rational mind of the settler. Her appearance is delayed because she is camouflaged into the background, a technique common in the depiction of Aboriginal people in colonial art who are often shown 'blending into the flora and fauna' (Jordan and Weedon 1995, p. 489). Without pausing and without a word being spoken she sits down and starts to kiss Tucker. The complete lack of dialogue suggests that they do not share a common language, and that her sexuality is outside language – it is "natural" and unashamed. It is the landscape, and in particular, the didgeridoo, that signals her body as Aboriginal. However, there is a crucial moment in this scene that indicates when she stops being a symbol of the exotic and becomes a heteronormative pornstar. At the precise moment she touches Tucker, the soundtrack abruptly changes. The didgeridoo is replaced by a synth piano soundtrack that is used throughout the film denoting sex scenes. At the literal point of colonial contact she is no longer Native, she is a porn actor.

This is the only scene where an Aboriginal character plays any part in the Australian pornoexotic films studied in Chapter 1, and its isolation from the main plot is achieved in two ways. First, it is the opening sex scene, often considered a warm up act in feature porn. Second, it is revealed at the end of the scene to have been a dream sequence. She represents a pure fantasy for Tucker, who at this point in the film has never visited Australia nor encountered an Aboriginal person. There is no attempt to make her real – she is framed as a mirage, as an erotic dream of the occident. The conventions of the pornoexotic do not allow her to exist outside of this dreamscape. This fantasy of Australia is necessarily juxtaposed with the reality of Tucker's visit to Australia, where all his sexual encounters are with non-Native settlers. Tucker's juxtaposition of sex dream and "reality" affirms the idea of Indigeneity as already extinct, only existing as an erotic fantasy of the past used to inspire settler futures.

The absence of Aboriginal people in porn

The self-identified Aboriginal body not only lacks any contemporaneity and self-determined sexual representative agency, but *any* representation in pornography. This raises questions as to why Aboriginal people are unrepresentable in contemporary porn. King, in writing on the first Aboriginal pornstar Nicci Lane, suggests that this marked an important shift in the reconciliation movement in Australia. King (2005, p. 523) proposed that Lane represented the start of 'imagining new kinds of interracial intimacy within the Australian public sphere'. However new images of Lane or other Aboriginal porn actors did not eventuate. This book emphasises that pornography's operative power is its distributive organisation – how it links explicit representations to non-pornographic hierarchies of power, race, property and nationalism. However, in this chapter I argue for the inverse power – the power to strip the distributive and relational work of representation from certain images. In this case the absence of Aboriginal people in pornographic networks, and how this refusal of representation is a deliberate neocolonial strategy that limits pornographic access and hence fantasies for settlers and Aboriginal people.

My discussion of *Outback Assignment* is a symptom of the absence of representations of Aboriginal people in pornography. The film was released over 25 years ago, featuring an Aboriginal character played by a non-Aboriginal actor, and yet no narrative porn with an Aboriginal character has been produced since. In heteroporn Aboriginal people are dead, and it is this message that is silently being distributed across relational representative networks every time a settler masturbates to porn. For the settler, as well as the Aboriginal audience, there is no "Native" Australian porn. The reasons for this absence, while many, are not abstract. They can be located in specific neocolonial measures introduced in Australia over the last two decades which have targeted Aboriginal people – most notable is *The Northern Territory National Emergency Response* (commonly referred to as The Intervention) from 2007–2010. The Intervention resulted in the military occupation of Aboriginal communities, the suspension of the *Racial Discrimination Act* (1975), the removal of customary law and cultural practices from the legal system, amongst other measures. While the suspension of the *Racial Discrimination Act* ended in 2010, many of the measures remain in place and will continue until 2022 (Altman and Russell 2012, p. 3).[11]

One of the lesser-known measures of The Intervention was the banning of pornography in Aboriginal communities. Signs at the entry of targeted Aboriginal communities announced the ban on pornography, stating: 'It is an offence to bring, possess, supply, sell or transport certain pornographic materials beyond this point'. The neo-colonial act of censorship in these communities reinstated stereotypes of Black people inflamed by pornography, incapable of consuming it responsibly. Mulholland (2016) refers to this as the most recent example of 'porn anxiety' in Australia that can be traced along racial and colonial histories. This prejudice was outlined in the *Little Children are Sacred Report* (Wild and Anderson 2007), commissioned by the Chief Minister of the Northern Territory and used to rationalise The Intervention. The report stated that the presence of pornography in these communities 'lead[s] inexorably to family and other violence and then on to sexual abuse of men and women and, finally, of children' (Wild and Anderson 2007, p. 9).[12] The ban marks a forceful policing of Aboriginal sexuality, denying access and ability to partake in sexual representations at a time when amateur pornography was redefining sexual expression and politics. It was a deliberate othering of Aboriginal communities, removing their voice from discourses of desire.[13] Preciado (2015) maintains that 'the audiovisual industry is the political editing room where public sexuality has been invented, produced, and broadcast as a visible image since the end of the nineteenth century', hence the exclusion of Aboriginal people from systems of pornographic representation was not about banning pornography, but about excluding Indigenous sexuality from being invented, edited, broadcast and politicised. It was an elimination strategy that understood pornography as not just representing sexuality but producing it.

As with previous attempts to ban pornography, the accusation in the report was that pornography normalises sexual violence, that it is used for grooming children and that it 'encourages them to act out the fantasies they've seen in magazines' (Wild and Anderson 2007, p. 200). Despite the police and military measures during The Intervention, there were no criminal prosecutions for child sexual abuse in the first six months (Korff 2006). Over two years the convictions for child sexual abuse involving Aboriginal perpetrators had 'barely changed' (Korff 2006) and over three years the rate of sexual assault charges had not increased (Altman and Russell 2012). As claims of an epidemic of sexual violence and child sexual abuse were the primary reasons for banning pornography, such findings suggest that there was not a crisis in the first place and that banning pornography has no effect on the incident rate of sexual crimes. In 2011 the Australian Government's own report into The

Intervention (Davis and Larkin 2011, p. 6) conceded that 'there is not enough evidence to know whether the NTNER pornography restrictions have been effective', and that it resulted in 'no evidence of behaviour change'.

Outside of the unsubstantiated correlation of pornography to sexual crimes there were only 47 pornography related offences recorded from the period 2007–2011 in these communities. The 2011 report suggests that such low numbers of incidents 'may be [because] there was not a lot of illegal use or distribution of pornography occurring' (Davis and Larkin 2011, p. 186). Of these offences, 95 per cent (42) were censorship offences (which are separate to child pornography offences). Considering that a significant amount of pornographic material freely available online would be classified as a censorship offence under Australian law, the small number of charges would relate to the heavy policing of laws that usually go unprosecuted (there was only one recorded censorship offence relating to pornography in the Northern Territory prior to The Intervention) rather than indicate any systemic criminal behaviour specific to these communities.

The Intervention's ban on pornography was also a measure to buttress settler sexuality, to ensure it remained purged of representations of Aboriginal sex, desires and bodies. The Intervention started in 2007, the same year *Pornhub* was launched. The launch of the site affirmed pornography as a white owned and consumed distribution network at a historic moment when pornography's sensible operation was dramatically expanding and redefining itself. The development of critical, pornographic representative power witnessed in post-pornography – with its representation of amateurs, women, queer and minoritarian positions and politics – is linked to the legislative, military and police response that ensured the Native/non-Native absolute at the centre of settler sexuality was preserved during these seismic technological and distributive changes. In other words, normative and antinormative porn expanded rapidly at the cost of the violent re-inscription of the Native/non-Native distinction.

Pornography's distributive power means that it was used as a convenient problem and its banning a convenient solution to The Intervention's goal of breaking Aboriginal people's cultural, kinship and physical connection to their land. Pornography and its deliberated association of Aboriginal people with deviant forms of settler sexuality, in this case child abuse, relied on a larger narrative that can be traced back to the start of settler colonisation. Angela Mitropoulos (2012, p. 143) argues that claims of child sexual abuse, creates a fear of disordered genealogy, and thus a demand for the reinstatement of the proper orders of property (e.g. the paternity invoked by state paternalism), for the legibility of property rights, and so their legitimate possession and transfer. In short, the accusation of endemic child sexual abuse is not outside the semantic field of the 'land grab' but a crucial part of its logic and legitimation.

Put another way, the activation of settler sexuality, and its representative form in pornography, was a continuation of land grabbing, justified on moral, sexual grounds and enacted through military, legal, cultural and representational violence. These issues cannot be separated because settler sexuality and settler colonisation were formed together and continue to be co-productive. And even if there is a difference between colonial and neocolonial sexual and property control structures, where disciplinary methods shift from death to life, the effect is the same. Moreton-Robinson (2015, p. 167) reminds us 'the exercising of patriarchal white sovereignty's right to let live or make live produces an early death for Indigenous people'. The banning of pornography, and just as importantly not banning pornography for settlers (or for sexually deviant settlers) is a form of property ownership. This will be explored more in the next chapter in relation to the cumshot. Here however, we can see how pornography's power is to draw on its exceptional status, as something that can hermetically cause problems, to disguise its actual distribution which ultimately leads to supporting private property in settler states. Hence its censorship, banning and restriction to Aboriginal people in Australia is also a restriction and delegitimisation of property and sovereignty claims.

(No) hope?

Attempting to locate possible pathways for the production and critique of Native porn within current heteroporn frameworks is not the goal for this chapter. Nor is my aim to end on an optimistic turn to recast settler sexuality as somehow capable of accommodating or being ruptured by Native porn. However, I do want to finish with a discussion of two types of porn found on *Pornhub* that sit uncomfortably in pure elimination narratives. The first is Native men either by themselves or with non-Native women and the second is Native couple heteroporn. There are 53 videos with titles that refer to a Native male, 26 of which are solo men masturbating, leaving 27 of

Native men with non-Native women. Of these videos, 22 have been uploaded by one user. The 27 videos have titles such as *Getting big native dick* and CHEATING WHITE HOUSEWIFE NEEDS HARD NATIVE COCK IN HER ASS, which align with titles in interracial porn, others that suggest Native men are incompatible with non-Native women SKINNY NATIVE CAN'T GET ERECTION FROM BIG WHITE GIRL and one that uses the language of ethnopornography *Navajo Savage Makes White Girl Suck and Swallow His Cum*. Following the logic of interracial porn, these videos could be considered as examples of "making Native" rather than making non-Native (although their titles suggest a general confusion as to the fecundity, pornographic narrative and purpose of Native men, rather than an identifiable stereotype; and the fact that there are so few of these texts, and the majority buried far into the results, suggest that any meaningful impact on the regime of the sensible seems very unlikely).

There are two users who uploaded Native couple heteroporn, both identifying as Native (*Nativethickdick* a 'Cree Indian' living in Canada, and *Vossauge85* a 'Cherokee EBCI Native American 1/2 Puerto Rican' living in the United Sates). *Voussauge85* uploaded one video titled CHEROKEE NATIVE AMERICAN COUPLE HARDCORE FUCKING, which is a two minute long, single shot of penetration with no talking and no faces shown. *Nativethickdick* has uploaded 22 videos across three usernames, some of which are re-uploads and 12 of which indicate a Native man and woman with titles such as *Native cock stretching native pussy*, *Native Pussy moaning being stretched by native*. All 22 videos are close ups focused on genitals, with no talking and no faces. All the videos are low quality and none are longer than two minutes. The 22 videos have only had a total of 29,776 views, on a site where 298 million videos are viewed each day (Pornhub 2018). It is hard to know how to analyse these videos, or indeed what to say about them, other than to say they exist which itself is exceptional.

The complete absence of porn titled as featuring only Native people that has been produced or uploaded by non-Natives suggests a total absence that is not only one of neglect, apathy and colonial violence, but one of fear. Rancière (2010, p. 50) tells us 'the protection of the person and his/her image thus produces an operation that is indissolubly political and ontological. It tends to subtract, along with a certain type of judgement and of political judgement, a part of the visible'. The protection, censorship and removal of Native porn is political (enshrining settler law) and ontological (reaffirming the extinction of Indigeneity). But we can ask what is feared in the settlers' judgement if they viewed Native porn? Kipnis (2014, p. 177) argues that 'pornography isn't viewed as having complexity, because its audience isn't viewed as having complexity, and this propensity for oversimplification gets reproduced in every discussion about pornography'. This oversimplification tends to reduce analysis of racialised porn to a singular affect and interpretation that ignores its unique operations. If Native porn could be simplified to the sexual subjugation of Indigenous people by settlers, then it is unlikely it would present a threat to settlers and its censorship would not be required. However because 'race aids pornographic protagonists in staging, enacting, and naming pleasures, even as it always already constrains protagonists' lexicons of desire' (Nash 2014, p. 3), Native porn would offer a type of spectatorship for Native audiences that is complex, and in part, future orientated. And for the settler, Native porn could result in somatic, relational, disruptive resonances with Indigenous sexual practices (real and imagined) that unsettle settler sexuality. The very fact such porn does not exist hints at its imagined power.

Notes

1 Some such examples (and by no means an exhaustive list) include Maddee Clark, Nayuka Gorrie, Hannah Bronte, Enoch Mailangi, Bridget Caldwell, Bhenji Ra, FAF SWAG, Club Ate.
2 Butler (2013, p. 22) was writing on Rodney King's assault by police in which she states,

> I do not mean to suggest by "white racist episteme" as static and closed system of seeing, but rather an historically self-renewing practice of reading which, when left uninterrupted, tends to extend its hegemonic force. Clearly, terms like "white paranoia" do not describe in any totalizing way 'how white people see,' but are offered here as theoretical hyperboles which are meant to advance a strategically aggressive counter-reading.

3 Ethnopornography's popularity presented a problem at the time of being too pornographic (or more likely too popular). As Povinelli (2002, p. 79) notes, 'several of Spencer and Gillen's colleagues provided graphically detailed accounts of Aboriginal sex acts and were subsequently accused of trafficking in pornography'.
4 Similar provisions exist in many former colonies and settler colonies. Remarkably the exact same phrase was used in *Native Courts (Amendment) Law, 1960* in Nigeria (cited in Asiedu-Akrofi 1989, p. 572) indicating the Australian High Court directly referenced former British colonies to define Native law, treating it as a universal concept across colonised countries. See Asiedu-Akrofi (1989).

5 This also contributes to the "loading" white porn actors are typically paid for sex scenes with Black men.
6 The racial codification and confusion witnessed here is systematic of the complexity of categorising racial ethnicity through colonial structures and technologies. This can be seen in blood quantums as measures of membership into Native Nations, and legal percentage classification of miscegenation in Australia. See Wolfe (2016).
7 There are other films such as *Indian Summers 1* and *2* (1991) which star Hyapatia Lee, but I have not been able to confirm details about these films. The four I have found are based on title and plot descriptions on IAFD.
8 Although the article has only 411 views, many of which have been mine over the course of this research.
9 Tuck and Yang (2012) note that appropriation is one of many performative, rhetorical and discursive strategies that settlers use to attempt to position themselves and their occupation as innocent.
10 This is not to say that there are no Aboriginal people working in the sex industry or in porn. This is an issue of how and why Aboriginal people are identified (or not identified) in porn.
11 The legislation that extends some of the measures – *Stronger Futures in the Northern Territory Act* – does not make any reference to the ban on pornography, however, appeals on the ban are made on a community-by-community basis to the Minster for Family Affairs, Housing, Community Services and Indigenous Affairs (*Senate Community Affairs Legislation Committee, Families, Housing, Community Services and Indigenous Affairs and Other Legislation Amendment (Restoration of Racial Discrimination Act) Bill 2009*).
12 Pornography was listed alongside of poor health, alcohol, drug abuse, gambling, unemployment, poor education and housing.
13 Further, the very fact such a ban was possible underlines the severe disadvantages of these communities, as the ban was only effective because of the general lack of access to the internet. If Aboriginal communities had access to the internet outside of publicly surveyed institutions, it would have made the ban a farce. Further to this, the report suggests that adults watched pornography in view of children, which the report itself states is a result of overcrowding of housing (Davis and Larkin 2011, p. 65).

3 The colonial cumshot

The cumshot is seemingly the most pornographic of gestures. It signifies the ending of the narrative and the end of narrative. Situated at 'the very limit of the visual', (Williams 1999, p. 101) its forensic treatment and biological focus makes its presentation explicit and obvious. The cumshot is material evidence of male orgasm and pleasure presented to the viewer. Anti-porn feminist critiques of heteroporn hold the cumshot as evidence of male pleasure predicated on female performance, and the material of that pleasure as designating or making dirty that which he owns (Dworkin 1995). In this definition and critique the cumshot is limited to the visualisation of male orgasm, necessitated by the misogynist and practical requirements of pornography. This restricted reading is stabilised by porn's own claims of its authenticity and indexicality. In contrast, this chapter defines the cumshot as an operation between different relations, gestures, materials, images and conditions. The cumshot is the representation of male orgasm in porn (cum as orgasm and material), it is the viewer at "home" masturbating and producing their own cum (material) with the pornographic representation, and it is the homosociality of male masturbators who engage in the cumshot as a mediated communal sex act. These three together produce the operation of the cumshot as a contemporary post-pornographic sex act, and for the purpose of this chapter, a heterosex act at the centre of settler sexuality.

When the cumshot is considered as a set of relations we can see that its distribution into the sensible is as an open, fluid symbol of productivity. Further, by positioning the cumshot as an expression of settler sexuality rather than located only in pornography, it can be revealed as an act of heterosex that connects masturbating male settlers with images. The cumshot authenticates hierarchies of gender, race, ownership, productivity and labour. It is strategically distributed into networks that validate private property, masculinity, whiteness and excessive production. The cumshot positions white male material production – cum as material and immaterial, something that can be seen and touched and an infinite, natural, alchemic resource coming from the body of the settler – as central to the colonial project. Unlike the preceding chapters, this chapter is an expansive argument that speculates how the cumshot can be reread through colonial structures and actions. Claiming that the cumshot is the most common form of heterosex for men in a settler colony is deliberately positioned as both simply factual and highly speculative, allowing for connections that are absurd and logical, funny and serious. I aim to write a theory of the cumshot in a way that reflects the properties of the cumshot itself. I am taking this approach to attempt access to the conspiratorial and material power it holds.

Locke's (2018) definition of property as a natural right is always a question of labour. For Locke the natural rights to property only apply to men who laboured in a particular way. Land that has no evidence of "labour" is not property, and men who do not "labour" are not eligible for natural rights. According to a Lockean understanding of property, the settler's blood, sweat and tears are by-products of the labour that makes his home. However, once the home is made, and settlement proclaims victory over internal frontiers, a neocolonial Lockean bodily substance can be found – cum. Cum is not a mere by-product of labour, but the intended product of the labour of masturbation. Cum as a neo-Lockean material cannot be separated from the cumshot because it is through the cumshot that the masturbating settler finds solidarity and signification. In this chapter I argue that the cumshot's fixated display of cum affirms heredity and productivity for the masturbating settler, providing evidence for the two dominant colonial defences of property. The cumshot is a neocolonial interactive domestic event that every day marks the settler's privilege and property as properly his. It operates across different ideological regimes of the colonial and neocolonial, biopolitical and pharmacopornographic, industrial and neoliberal, material and post-pornographic to be both a fluid symbol of productivity and the literal substance of white futurity. It offers contradictory authentications of colonisation that attempt to naturalise the white supremacist work of settlement.

Defining the cumshot

The cumshot is the combination of two self-reflexive, solipsistic characteristics of orgasm and porn – an orgasm as defined by 'who feels it, knows it' (Jagose 2013) and porn as by 'who sees it, knows it' (Stewart 1964).[1] This seems to leave little room for defining or questioning the representation of orgasm, as it is phenomenologically and visually self-evident. The cumshot is used as a potent symbol and example for a range of different ideological positions, however it has largely escaped careful description and definition, with the focus on what it means (for the actors, for the viewers, for society) rather than what it is and what it does. In heteroporn the cumshot consists of a sequence which typically includes the following: the withdrawal of the penis from a mouth, vagina or anus; manual stimulation of the penis by the actor; close up of a male face; close up of a penis ejaculating; semen landing on an intended subject (usually a woman); excess semen landing on unintended object/s; the semen as it moves after landing; and a woman enjoying or rejecting the semen. The cumshot sequence may contain some or all of these shots, or additional shots, but importantly it is not completed in one singular image; rather, it is a variable sequence, made up of cuts, closeups, specific angles, gestures and most importantly audience participation.[2] It is a shorthand term for a set of conventions which can be critically analysed and are historically locatable. Considering the cumshot only as a visualisation of male orgasm does not reveal the significance or reality of the cumshot in heteroporn. The cumshot is post-pornographic – it is participatory, integrated into domestic life and heterosex, and motivated by desires and privilege that extend beyond and even bypass sexual gratification.

Precisely when the cumshot emerges is unclear, in part, because there is no universal definition. Representations of disembodied penises ejaculating have a long history with examples of graffiti, domestic images, and religious, totemic images and narratives dating back at least to the Ancient Egyptians.[3] In heteroporn and erotica there is little evidence of it before the twentieth century. In modern pornography it appears as a specific subject in drawings of gay men from the 1920s, which Cindy Patton (1989, p. 106) states was used to 'draw some narrative closure to the sketches'. In heteroporn the cumshot was present by accident rather than design in stag films in the first half of the twentieth century. As Williams (1999, p. 93) notes:

where the earlier short, silent stag films occasionally included spectacles of external ejaculation (in some cases inadvertently), it was not until the early seventies, with the rise of the hard-core feature, that the money shot assumed the narrative function of signalling the climax of a genital event.

By the 1970s, the cumshot had emerged as a trope of heteroporn largely due to the commercial success of *Deep Throat* (1972). From this point on the cumshot became compulsory and signalled the end of the narrative and fucking – as Ziplow's 1977 manual for making porn instructs 'if you don't have the cum shots you don't have a porno picture' (p. 34). The reasons for its rapid ascension in heteroporn range from health concerns (in the 1970s sexual health tests were slow and still not common in the porn industry, and the cumshot was seen as a safe explicit representation, allowing for the use of condoms in penetration scenes) to visual preference (it was easier to film, and required less of the male body in shot) to signalling to the male viewer to finish masturbating (Delacroix in Hay 2016). Perhaps the most significant historical fact of the cumshot is that it has stayed largely unchanged for the last 40 years, both in form and frequency. Even as the access, methods and distribution of heteroporn have transformed, the cumshot remains a dominant feature in the post-pornographic era. It is the limit of the explicit that pornography has not transcended. Despite being a recent visual invention, it has become the full stop of heteroporn. Without it, the pornographic text is seemingly incomplete.

Analysis of the cumshot sequence reveals how it is constructed to appear as if it is documentary, footage that affirms the connection between orgasm and ejaculation. Focusing on the display of a close up of the male face in orgasmic ecstasy and the close up of a penis ejaculating demonstrates one of the most obvious constructions for this connection. Despite narratively describing the same event, they are often two separate events, as many porn shoots only have one camera, so filming both closeups simultaneously is impossible. The male cum face is not pleasure, but the performance of pleasure shot independently of ejaculation. The facial expression is not affective proof, but a signal of what is to follow. Similarly, the close up of a penis ejaculating is not exactly what it appears to be. Most porn shoots are very short, demanding multiple sex scenes and cumshots performed in a day.[4] The necessity for cum to be the signifier of male orgasm means that the porn industry has to provide substitutes and trickery to achieve a seemingly endless supply for its actors. There are a variety of strategies used, from stand-in penises to artificial cum that is pumped through hidden tubes, to post-production enhancements.[5] Cinematic conventions apply to ensure the expectations of continuity – that cum is seen to be produced and projected by the orgasming male subject – hold. I am not suggesting the cumshot is fake, but neither is it objectively real; it is a visual sequence that relies on cinematic techniques to convey authenticity.

The cumshot is variously described as 'not merely [a] reference [of] phallic pleasure – it seems it is phallic pleasure' (Tuck 2003, p. 271), 'mechanical "truth" of bodily pleasure' (Williams 1999, p. 101), 'irrefutable proof of genetic maleness' (Faludi 1995, p. 68), 'material reality that confirms men's pleasure' and that 'it can only confess to its own physical truth' (Aydemir 2007, pp. 72, 138).[6] These descriptions do not account for the practical constraints, trickery, framing and visual codes that make the cumshot a construction. It also sets up an opposition between male and female orgasm, which within heteroporn is not so much a biological opposition as a structuring principle. The woman's orgasm is expected to be fake, as her designation as a sex worker is accepted (if not required), whereas the male is expected to overcome the work. The cumshot's indexical deception is no doubt one reason for its persistence, it remains the thing that the audience can hold onto as singularly real. The fucking is, of course, also real too although simultaneously histrionically performed. It is only the cumshot that seemingly is a moment in which the male actor becomes fooled by his own performance and offers the audience a "real" event that exceeds its context. For the audience it is an irrefutable orgasm, whose pleasure is often immediately confirmed by their own. The cumshot is the anchor for a genre that is consumed a-lineally, distractedly and participatory.[7] It can solve any narrative problems, any filming mishaps, any acting mistakes – it is the "money shot" for these reasons. The framing of the cumshot as the real, explicit, degrading, terminal gesture at the limit of heteroporn occludes the fact that in most instances the cumshot is a product of male masturbation. Steve Garlick (2012, p. 307) recognises the cumshot as 'accomplished via an act of masturbation', and further Murat Aydemir (2007, p. 128) notes 'the simple fact that the male performers usually masturbate themselves to climax is easily missed'. Reconfiguring the cumshot through the lens of masturbating actor and audience is essential to analysing its formal and critical characteristics as authenticating masculinity through masculinity, and addresses why, as Aydemir (2007, p. 112) argues, the cumshot 'may actually be the place where pornography gets stuck rather than where it culminates?'

The cumshot gets stuck because of its two contradictory representative imperatives, which Annamarie Jagose (2013, p. xvi) summarises in the following way: 'the alleged indexicality of the representational capture of embodied orgasm is crucial and crucial also to the subsequent crises of authenticity and objectivity that inevitably attend attempts to stabilise orgasm in the field of the visible'. The cumshot holds orgasm to be something stable, something provable, self-regulated and produced, visible and material – or to put it simply, it holds orgasm to be masculine. Yet its naturalisation of masculinity as materially and representationally fixed is achieved through a construction that cannot sustain its own indexical claim. The cumshot marks an end point, but only to immediately demand another. The cumshot may be the limit of pornography, but it is a limit anxiously repeated again and again because it feels empty, hollow and in some sense (visually, emotionally, affectively) fake. For Aydemir (2007, p. 111, xx), 'the repetition of the cum shot articulates a desire for the entropy, fading, or cessation of the narrative. Through iteration, meaning exhausts or voids itself in a dynamic that is recessive and regressive rather than forward-moving', such that 'ejaculation becomes the instance where the story halts, freezes, coagulates, fans out, digresses, or drearily repeats itself'. For Perter Brooks (1992) it represents failure, for Williams (1999) it is a perversion of male pleasure, and Paul Smith (1988) suggests that it might not mean anything in particular. The cumshot is a very loaded symbol, but the more it is examined the less it seems to tell us.

If we consider the operation of the cumshot beyond the context of pornography, then its anxious, empty repetition is part of the broader garbled integration of heterosex and culture.[8] The cumshot is both overdetermined and empty, definitive and anxious, natural and excessive, authentic and constructed. Positioning these dialectics as operating within settler colonisation reveals a similarity in strategies that attempt to naturalise and authenticate heterosex and colonisation through culture, law, work, pleasure and property. This is not a coincidence as settler sexuality describes the co-dependent development of heterosexuality and colonisation. Hence the most obvious connection between the cumshot and settler colonisation is its visualisation of settler sexuality. Taking the cumshot as an index of authentic male pleasure provides the male settler with evidence that authentic experience is possible on stolen land and from within heterosexuality. This direct connection will be explored first before destabilising this connection to examine the cumshot's more enmeshed and complex operation as material evidence of settler labour.

"Natural" sexuality

The construction of settlers' sex, desires and orgasms as "natural" is central to justifications for colonialism. I am interested in the effect of settler sexuality on the settler, and how they adopt white supremacist desire as normative and natural. This desire is primarily located in white, hetero-men and its most common expression and representation is cum. The "natural" claim of settler sexuality uses desire as its authenticating framework, and the embodied, unquestionable, material, "natural" orgasm as its evidence. Halperin (1994, p. 34) claims there is 'no orgasm without ideology', and the orgasms of settler sexuality are ideologically constructed and experienced. This is to say that the experience of orgasm is used to justify settler ideology, and is produced through the consumption of ideology, the most direct form of which is pornography. Heteroporn is an obvious example of Warner's (1993, p. xx) definition of heterosexual culture as 'think[ing] of itself as the elemental form of human association, as the very model of intergender relations, as the indivisible basis for all community, and as the means of reproduction without which society wouldn't exist'. The fucking and cumming in pornography go beyond other forms of heterosexual culture by being able to treat the 'means of reproduction' as documentary rather than metaphor, presenting itself as elemental in its medium, expression and consumption. In this way sex, heteroporn, masturbation and orgasm are made "natural" through a deliberate conflation of colonial heterosexual culture and the individual's desires. For the settler there is no way to disentangle sexual desire from colonial desire. This conflation can be traced to the first conceptualisations of settler colonies. The Commission to settle Australia, written on behalf of King George III was presented to Governor Phillip in 1787. The draft Commission discusses the importance of settler sexuality and instructs Phillip 'to promote matrimonial Connexion, which must upon many accounts be productive of great advantage to the settlement, as well as to the Interests and Happiness of the Individuals' (Phillip 2010, p. 8).[9] Here individual desires expressed as sex within marriage are simultaneously productive to and of settlement. Desire expressed towards colonial goals comes with the promise of profit and happiness for the individual settler. This same logic continues today, sustaining the belief in settler sexuality as the only form of desire that has productive nationalist and individual outcomes.

There is no orgasm without history, culture, narrative or imagery. The settler cums with, alongside, and onto these things. As discussed in Chapter 2, pornography's appearance, categorisation and distribution follows from the invention of settler sexuality and its privileging of the white body as the normative standard. Pornography's racialised valuation of sex, desire and people is directly linked to producing value in national and settler structures. Although McKee (1999, p. 179) states 'porn [is] not a genre obviously associated with projects of nation-building', this separation is due to the success of porn's "naturalisation". The Australian National Film and Sound Archive only holds 220 pornographic titles, the majority of which are from the 1990s and appear with brief, descriptive text. Hidden amongst 3 million items, the National Archive's inability to recognise pornography as in anyway part of nation building is a deliberate naturalisation of settler sexuality.

Seen as a product of settler sexuality, all pornography is colonial and all cumshots are the colonisation of orgasm. Any one cumshot maybe more or less supportive of a colonial state, but all have the potential to be used by the settler to affirm their claim – which is why Indigenous people, and Indigenous cum is the ultimate taboo in pornography. As Buckley (1983, p. 9) points out, in settler colonies 'the land is a breeding ground and a killing ground', and this dual act echoes through the cumshot, in the bodies whose reproductive material is represented, in the bodies that are erased, and in the 'white-dominated representational economy' (Nash 2014, p. 2) that distributes the cumshot across capacious colonial networks of productivity and sovereignty.

The masturbating settler

The viewer masturbating at home is the part of the cumshot which is rarely discussed, but it is integral to its operation within settler sexuality. 'The cum shot', writes Aydemir (2007, p. 140), 'becomes most real or authentic when and if three instances of "shooting" appear to happen simultaneously: the actor ejaculating on the set, the camera capturing this ejaculation as it happens, and the viewer coming at home'. The viewer is not just a viewer, but in ejaculating with the image is active in producing a post-pornographic, cultural orgasm. The cumshot is most "real" and most "authentic" when these three "shootings" occur because the viewer invests in the image and produces what he perceives to have witnessed. The cumshot appears to tell us over and over that a real event has occurred, and we know this because we have explicitly seen it, and simultaneously, we have felt it. The three shootings generate a reflexive loop, affirming the image, the material and the orgasm as real. The authentication value of one system is used as evidence for the other – the material of the viewer's cum as proof of orgasm, the orgasm as proof of their desire for heteroporn, and the image as proof of the indexicality of their cum. For hetero-men I argue it is likely that masturbating with the cumshot is their most common expression of heterosex.

If we understand masturbation as the primary expression of settler sexuality, then modes of masturbation such as the cumshot are not representations of, or substitutes for, sex.[10] Once post-pornographic masturbation is taken into account, penial-vaginal intercourse loses its dominance as the most significant, frequent or symbolic of heterosex acts. Jagose (2013, p. 178) states that 'the critical value accorded to certain sex acts is often in the service of systems of discrimination more ideological than erotic'. Here we might understand the ideological operation of coupled heterosex to be its public normativity and its centrality to heterosexual culture.[11] Male masturbation operates differently and despite being widely distributed into the sensible through the cumshot, it appears to have not publicly accumulated such "critical value". What is strange about male masturbation is how often it is discussed (joked about, referenced, alluded to) yet how little it is analysed and taken seriously. It is spoken about, and enjoyed amongst men, but in various tones and registers that are assumed to have no educational, social, economic, national or reproductive value. A lack of attention to male masturbation in porn studies may be because of its Foucauldian tradition that sees porn's operation as one of difference between audience and image – the search for a scientific truth (gendered or racial) that is promised but undelivered in the representation of explicit sex.[12] Nash (2014) points out that this assumes a white male spectator and precludes porn's potential to be something that audiences might identify with rather than against, and take pleasure in that identification. To extend this critique, it also means that a white male audience who invests in representations that are similar to him (the cumshot as about male orgasm, rather than female "pleasure") are considered to have limited hermeneutic value. As such, masturbation is everywhere and nowhere. Masturbation is widely distributed, but it rarely interacts with the distribution of coupled heterosex. Like pornography, its distribution is through patriarchal, white networks that deliberately disguise its reach and effect. Taking male masturbation, and its contemporary manifestation in and through the cumshot as having serious critical and common value, might suggest that it is not so much coupled heterosex that is naturalised and protected in settler sexuality, but male masturbation. The white male who cums with white male porn actors is potentially the most normative expression of settler heterosex.

I discussed the specific operation of pornoexotic mate-sex in Chapter 1. Here it is expanded to include the male viewer, who watches a man masturbate while he masturbates. This sex act is between an isolated body, image and an assumed community of white masturbators. The masturbating viewer negotiates media, finding places to pause, repeat, skip, imitate and finally ejaculate. It is assumed that the dismembered penis of the cumshot becomes that of the viewer, who through point of view perspective takes the position of the actor and embodies the penis. As Patton (1989, p. 105) states, the cumshot is framed so that 'the viewer is tightly positioned as the person who owns the penis'. But this transformation is not necessarily so "clean", it is far more likely to be registered as another penis than confused for the viewer's own, because it is a framed image and the viewer's own penis is also visible and being touched. The assumption that the viewer lacks complexity and visual intelligence is a dangerous stereotype of pornography which obscures its operation and power. The actual relationship between imaged penis and the viewer's penis can be understood through Jacques Derrida's notion of the example, where the actor's imaged penis is both very specific yet can be substituted without recognition. This is literally true in the porn production itself where stand-in penises are used, without the audience's awareness of the switch. It is also true of the viewer, who sees the imaged penis as not theirs, but it could become theirs. For Derrida (1998, p. 47) 'the example is not substitutable; but at the same time the same aporia always remains: this irreplaceability must be exemplary, that is replaceable. The irreplaceable must allow itself to be replaced on the spot'. In the cumshot the feeling is specific (it is a specific penis that is not mine), but also general (a brotherhood of white penises) that includes their own, the actors and other masturbators as endlessly interchangeable.

The fact that a male viewer masturbating with a masturbating male actor through the cumshot is constructed as unquestionably and explicitly hetero reveals that sex between men is central to heterosexuality and, by extension, to settler sexuality.[13] It is this "real", "authentic" experience between body and image that becomes the quotidian expression of male settler desire. Aydemir (2007, p. 149) elaborates, 'the fiction that feature hard core [porn] passes off for real is the privilege of ejaculation, and hence, of masculinity, while dissimulating its precious construction and maintenance'. The construction and maintenance of whiteness and masculinity in settler colonies is dissimulated through the cumshot, in the iterative and interactive act that aims to naturalise watching white men masturbating and cumming. The cumshot marks the spot of an experience that is constructed as unquestionably male, authentic, white, visible, represented, material and pleasurable. It is not only ejaculation, but ejaculate which is privileged in the cumshot, as Hallam (2004, p. 72) reminds us, 'ejaculate is not only the result of the moment of orgasm, but it is an articulation of pleasure, a reminder, and a remnant'. Its persistence after orgasm in pornography and masturbation is a locator, a marker that is touched even if only in its removal.[14] Describing the strange normativity that surrounds the orgasm, Lauren Berlant (2009, p. 262) tells us that it:

> seems to make you shatteringly different than your ego was a minute ago, but in another minute you are likely to be doing something utterly usual, like pissing, whispering, looking away, or walking into the kitchen and opening the refrigerator door.

Cum connects these two moments through material persistence – the orgasmic moment followed by the act of cleaning up its material trace. The shatteringly different and utterly usual are tied together through the material conditions of private property and cum.

The masturbating male understands that the conditions of property, consumerism, hetero-relationship and coupled heterosex have produced and insulated a space for his participation in the cumshot. These conditions provide the space for the male viewer to masturbate and ejaculate in private with other men (the imaged male pornstar and the imagined community of male viewers).[15] By framing male orgasm and cum as natural and showing how they can be produced within settler structures and through settler porn means that no matter how performed sex is, the relationship is, the family is, the state is, there can be no denying the reality of what they have produced. The cumshot is not simply the retrospective authentication of settler structures because the cumshot's profit and privilege is not tied to the *authenticity* of these structures. The acting in porn can be obvious without affecting the fucking and the fucking can be histrionic without affecting the cumshot, so too can settler structures be performed without their violent impacts and production of privilege being any less real. The male settler who masturbates with the cumshot can conceive of most of his life, including coupled heterosex as performative without this performance being registered as a failure because it maintains the location of his experience of privilege.[16] The cumshot is one of his most frequent and evidentiary experiences of privilege.

Coupled heterosex

Coupled heterosex in a settler colony can be understood as performance and work in a variety of different ways. The heterosex depicted in pornography is primarily concerned with getting the male close to orgasm, but it does not often, in itself produce the orgasm. In porn, orgasm is produced by masturbation, and heterosex is either the performance of straightness before male orgasm, or a technique for approaching it. In porn and in coupled heterosex, this phenomenon is widely accepted for straight women who engage in vaginal intercourse, as orgasm is often independent from intercourse. However, the cumshot demonstrates that for men the orgasm is similarly separated from intercourse. By de-emphasising coupled heterosex, its failures can be framed as largely incidental to pleasure and desire (although not performativity) in settler sexuality. While it can be pleasurable, it is not required to be – it can fail without threatening heteronormativity. As Jagose (2013, p. 194) points out,

> Although it has frequently been misrecognized as just such a strategy, drawing attention to the public failures of heterosexuality is not in itself an unsettling or destabilizing gesture, as is readily evidenced by the failure of those failures to register significantly against heterosexuality's social value. Far from being the end of the road, or even a malfunction, failure is a part of modern heterosexuality's support system, buoyed by aspiration, consolation, and optimism: the everyday bricolage of emotional making do.

Illustrating the failures is part of heterosex's normative performative work. Its failures are central to its critical value; they produce obstacles to be overcome in narratives that ultimately corroborate normativity's naturalising claim. This work is public, taking place in advice columns, films, documentaries, couples' therapy and law courts and has bares little relation to actual coupled heterosex. The *private* failure of coupled heterosex is not significant in itself, as Duncombe and Marsden (1993) argue, heteronormative couples can be seen as engaging in sex work, that is an extension of the emotional work required to maintain what they perceive to be normative experience. Privilege and profit are the reward for being heteronormative and this requires sex work, rather than heterosex being the reward for the work of the colonial, straight subject. For white male settlers, the gendered difference that labels their masturbation, ejaculation and consumption of the cumshot as normative are additional rewards.

In this analysis of the cumshot's relation to settler sexuality, there is still a slippage between orgasm, ejaculate and pleasure that appears to be inextricable from the cumshot. Desire and pleasure compel the cumshot into existence, providing an ideological outlet for men to experience pleasure from within colonial frameworks. However as has been demonstrated, for porn actors the cumshot is not always, or even often an orgasm. For the viewer, their act of masturbation should not be considered as always pleasurable, nor should we say that ejaculation and orgasm are the same thing. It is possible to ejaculate without orgasm; or to put it another way to orgasm without pleasure.[17] The viewer may masturbate for many reasons, for the privilege, for the privacy, for the productivity, for identitarian affirmation, for entertainment, for self-expression, for the ascesis, for the image-based sociality, for the ejaculate, for the activity. Pleasure is one of many possible reasons, the decision to masturbate is plural, it requires spatio-temporal privilege that means masturbating to orgasm is a demonstration of a set of conditions, rather than a suspension of them.

The notion that orgasm can perform a set of conditions rather than be an expression of pleasure, is explored by Jagose (2013, pp. 205–6) in her assertion that the fake orgasm is a positive cultural practice that 'emerges from a set of culturally specific circumstances as a widespread sexual observance, a new disposition or way of managing one's self in sexual relations'. For Jagose (2013, p. 202) this is specific to fake female orgasm as producing an alterity that is not one of erotic dissemblage but one of solidarity within straight narratives that 'indexes a future lived strenuously as a disappointing repetition in the present'.[18] The "fake" or unpleasurable male orgasm similarly generates an alterity that connects straight men in a manner that reinforces the repetition of the present, not as a disappointment, but as a consolidation of the conditions of power and privilege they collectively experience. In the following section, I focus on the decision to masturbate and cum with the cumshot as a decision to work that ties together settler sexuality, settler labour and property rights.

"Natural" work

The decision of the audience and porn actors to *work* to produce the cumshot can be understood as the many jobs and performances required to produce the broader conditions that support the cumshot's appearance. However, considering the cumshot itself as work, rather than the reward for work, is less evident. As discussed above, for the porn actor the cumshot is not a moment when he loses himself, it is a moment when he feels the orgasm approach and takes control of it, transforming the orgasm into a designed expression, a contractual act that is judged by how well it is performed. It is often the control not to cum, as ejaculation is a hindrance to the construction of the cum sequence. For the audience, their role in the cumshot is similarly designed. It requires a conspiracy of privacy – the manufacture of reasons to withdraw from the family, the relationship and shared domestic space. Once secluded their participation is choreographed with the actor. The audience has to cum with the cumshot (or pause or repeat it), because there is nothing after it. The cumshot is a regulation of ejaculation for actors and audience. I propose that by thinking of the cumshot as the work of the actor and audience to produce cum reveals how it is distributed into systems of settler work rather than pleasure. In particular, considering the cumshot as work demonstrates how the institutionalised work of colonisation is naturalised into "labour". I will first outline how work becomes labour in a settler colony before situating cum as a bodily production that the settler identifies as evidence of the labour of his hands.

To work in settler colonies has layered meaning and is not the simple translation of a patriotic effort to build a nation into a series of productive tasks. I used the term "work" to describe actions that are governed and categorised by people.[19] This is to make clear that the work of colonisation is a project that should be separated from the labour of staying alive. A settler colony deliberately conflates these by suggesting that the work of colonisation is also labour – narratives of survival in a harsh environment are an attempt to naturalise the actions of the settler on stolen land. The focus on performing labour in a colony disguises the new forms of actual labour that these processes inflict on Indigenous people. The history of colonial art is replete with images of work/labour, where the white body is under threat. Their perseverance, their blood, sweat and tears, is required rather than requested. Paintings of colonial labour propose it as the only work possible, despite the thousands of years of different, successful work by First Nations people that such images erase.

Indigenous work constitutes the background of these paintings which flattens time, flora, fauna and people into a plane waiting for colonial labour.[20] The imaged incompatibility of colonial and Indigenous land management is precisely the point, as the conflation of colonial work/labour follows Locke's "natural rights". The settler's "labour for survival" is tied to his "natural rights" – both appeal to a universal "truth" to conceal the gendered, colonial and class distinctions that structure what counts as labour and property. Cheryl Harris (1992, pp. 1727–8) articulates this process in relation to America, characterising such labour as white, whereby 'the Founders ... so thoroughly embraced Lockean labour theory as the basis for a right of acquisition because it affirmed the right of the New World settlers to settle on and acquire the frontier'. She goes on to say that 'as the forms of racialized property were perfected, the value and protection extended to whiteness increased' (p. 1728). In the Australian context Henry Reynold's (2003, pp. 26–7) states that 'Locke's ideas were used to justify the dispossession of the Aborigines because they had apparently not mixed their labour with the soil'. Locke's labour theory is used to bind property, whiteness, male exertion and settlement together in a definition intended to exclude Indigenous people.

The connection between Locke, colonialism, cultivation and bodily fluids is explored by Marianna Papastephanou and Zelia Gregoriou (2014). They argue that the colonial child's "natural learning" is their toil, evidenced by their blood and sweat. This toil is rewarded when the child becomes an adult – the child becomes a citizen and their labour becomes their property. The child and his parents' toil to cultivate the land, and it is this familial, generational toil that affirms their "natural right" to property. Their colonial blood and sweat mix with the soil, materially binding their body to agriculture. Locke (2018, para. 27) describes this process as central to property, claiming that cultivation is proof that 'he hath mixed his labour with [nature] ... and thereby makes it his property'. Bodily fluids produced from the "right" type of labour are literally mixed with nature to produce property.[21]

However, the problem of this sweaty "labour" is well known to a settler colony. The recognition of its absurdity forms undercurrents in cultural narratives. The search for authenticity in uncanny Euromimicry, or what Reynold's (2002, p. 42) refers to as the 'existential absurdity' of colonial work, is ever present. The paradox of settler colonisation, that Clemens and Pettman (2010, p. 148) ascribes as the desire to both 'possess land and to leave it' is in constant conflict with the need to naturalise the colonial work of making property.

Public images of colonisation are excessive in how they mythologise work as labour, and through overidentification white settlers continue to consume these narratives. However, the disparity between cultural expressions of labour and the actual lived experience of settlers is hard to ignore. In as much as Tourism Australia advertisements are consumed with pride and insecurity from locals, so too are paintings of farmers cultivating the land with their hands. They are icons, but not documentary evidence of Lockean labour, nor images that reflect the contemporary life of the settlers. Further, the settler is constantly confronted by the violence of colonisation, and their active or complicit part in this violence. The history of this violence is not recorded in the cannon of settler colonial images and hence a gap opens between publicly acceptable images of settler labour and the daily violence that structures their property claim. This gap is extended in neocolonisation where different forms of work (and violence) are required. Most of this work does not produce blood, sweat or tears which are mixed with the soil as evidence of their natural rights and productivity. A new bodily material is required for the settler to fulfil his Lockean duty. I propose that the cumshot as I have defined it, functions as a new binding of property and the settler's body through the "labour" of masturbation.

The work of his hand

The contemporary white, male settler struggles to defend his Lockean natural rights through bodily exertion. The middle class neocolonial male settler does not toil, nor till, nor tend to his property. The labour of his body has largely been outsourced to cleaners, gardeners, builders and his bodily exertion transferred to leisure and health activities. Yet the bodily act of masturbation, and the mediated sociality of the cumshot remains an act that is distinctly his and occurs on his property. Locke's (2018, para. 27) definition of labour can be easily applied to masturbation,

> The Labour of his Body, and the Work of his Hands, we may say, are properly his. Whatsoever then he removes out of the State that Nature hath provided, and left it in, he hath mixed his Labour with, and joyned to it something that is his own, and thereby makes it his Property.

The labour of his body, and literally the work of his hand in masturbation are understood as 'properly his'. This is a claim to bodily autonomy, identity and privacy attained through the 'work of his hands'. During masturbation what he removes from nature is not natural resources, but "natural sexuality" that *requires* cultivation to be properly his. He mixes porn with his "labour" and the evidence he is left with is "his own", transforming exertion into tangible material. The masturbatory cumshot is the triumph of "man over nature" – he labours to turn "natural" desire into property through the consumption of pornography and through the production of material cum.[22] As Garlick (2012, p. 319) argues the 'endeavour to gain control over the body marks the masturbatory character of contemporary pornography as an aspect of a broader project of masculinity as the (self)-control over nature'. The self-control of the settler's body is ultimately the control of material production, witnessed as coming from the settler, and controlled by the settler's hand.

Tuck and Yang (2012, p. 6) argue the settler is defined by his excessive production, they state:

> he can only make his identity as a settler by making the land produce, and produce excessively, because 'civilization' is defined as production in excess of the 'natural' world (i.e. in excess of the sustainable production already present in the Indigenous world).

The cumshot is an exemplar of the excessive production of the settler, it appears to be without purpose, being produced only to be wiped away. Cum does not make the land excessively produce in the way that blood and sweat are seen as productive of agriculture. Cum is excessively productive for contemporary settlers for whom land is now domestic and suburban and their bio-reproduction controlled and limited. It is nothing but excessive material, being produced in excess of (and crucially not as a replacement for) its bio-reproductive duty. The suburban home is the male settler's excessive, domestic cum factory. Every day that he cums with the cumshot he marks, and in so doing, makes his home. The labour of masturbating and the production of cum is part of homemaking that claims its "natural right" in its excessive, repetitive material productivity. The cumshot combines the settler's cum with colonial representative networks to connect his specific production to the collective production of colonial male masturbators.

The cumshot is an image, it is a network, it is a culture, a gesture, but it is also a material. Mar (2016) argues that the structures of colonisation cannot be thought outside of the material, and cum is a material whose colonial agency extends beyond its bio-reproductive potential. Cum's operation through the cumshot has evaded critique because it is considered wasteful, entertainment and hidden. However, if we reframe these characteristics as excessively productive, laborious and protected then cum is an "authentic" material which cultivates masculinity, whiteness and property. Crucially, the "cumshot as work" judged by a material outcome means that there is no affective, embodied test to confirm the cumshot or the colonial claim. The miserable colonist who masturbates without orgasmic transcendence still successfully produces colonial material. Aydemir (2007, p. 161), referencing Williams construction of the orgasm in pornography, notes that what is often missed is how 'tersely and flatly, how devoid of fun, the male, ejaculations in porn are shown'. The cumshot without pleasure (for the actors and viewers) avoids any cliched risk of alterity that is associated with "ground shaking" orgasm. The worked out cumshot reinforces labour and associated material production as the only requirements to defend his property claim – and the material produced in this defence has a unique colonial value. Cum's ultimate value as a neo-Lockean, neocolonial material is that it can operate as a rigid substance of white futurity *and* as an abstract, fluid marker of excessive productivity. This cum can only be constructed as having this dual value because of the cumshot – the representative network that affirms and distributes his bio-reproductive material as an expansive and adaptive marker.

The neocolonial cumshot

I have described the cumshot as fake, authentic, material, image, work, pleasure, heterosex and heteroporn. While the central claim of this chapter is that the cumshot is material (and the representation of material), this is because beyond its literal reproductive futurity, cum has not been unpacked for its colonial materiality, especially in relation to masturbation and pornography. The complex dialectics of the cumshot are a result of different regimes operating at the same time: neocolonial and colonial, industrial and neoliberal, biopolitical and pharmacopornographic regimes produce settler colonial identity. The contemporary settler's cum and the cumshot are an invention of the neocolonial, pharmacopornographic and post-pornographic era, but they are also structured by legacies of biopower and colonisation. These different regimes operate together, and often in conflict with one another. In this chapter I have focused on settler sexuality and labour, but I wish to briefly outline the cumshot's connections to other global discourses on masturbation and pornography. This is in no way a comprehensive account, but rather to demonstrate that my focus on colonisation is not outside of these discourses. They are just as implicated as colonisation, precisely because we cannot think of colonisation independently from them. My aim has been to decentre the critique of the cumshot to start with the settler and reveal their lack of innocence in these global discourses. The male settler is not a periphery figure whose masturbation is directed by distant regimes of control clumsily repurposed for their context. The masturbating settler is productive of these regimes in a very direct way.

If the cumshot is a particular social and cultural form of male masturbation then it appears to be an exemplar of biopower where 'basic biological features of the human species became the object of a political strategy, of a general strategy of power' (Foucault 2007, p. 1). However, historically masturbation has not typically been considered as biopower because of its "dangerous" relationship to orgasm and its perceived waste of "life". Its prohibition rather than control was favoured, and as Foucault (1984, p. 79) writes 'the crusade against masturbation translated the arrangements of the restricted family ([made up of] parents, children) into a new technology of power-knowledge'. It was *anti*-masturbation that structured power-knowledge in insulated family units. Robert Darby (2005, p. 14) notes that masturbation was discouraged because it disrupted 'the central aim of nineteenth-century sexual medicine [which] was to control and regulate the penis, to make it more predictable and better behaved'. Similarly, Leo Bersani (2009, p. 103) claims 'the ... body, more specifically the penis, disciplines the hand that would rule it'. Interestingly, Foucault addresses masturbation primarily in relation to children's sexual education, alluding to it as a problem of maids and servants who were feared to be masturbating the children under their care. Here masturbation is a social sexual activity, not something the child discovers in isolation. The prohibition on masturbation arose from a fear of race and class contamination. As Stoler (1995, p. 18) claims, writing in reference to Foucault, that:

> the colonial variant of that discourse on children and their sexual desires was more about the cultural transgressions of women servants and native mothers than about children themselves, less about the pedagogy surrounding children's sexuality than the racialisation of it.

In the eighteenth and nineteenth century, masturbation was pathologised both as an act between bodies and as a caressing of the self.

The sociality of masturbating we witness in the cumshot has a historical precedent, however its racialisation has been inverted from a fear of impurity within the family home, to an affirmation of whiteness and masculinity across domestic spaces and representational regimes.

In the first half of the twentieth century male masturbation was seen less as a perversion and more as a waste under a capitalist logic. As Greg Tuck (2009, p. 86) notes 'as a moment of pure consumption masturbation seems to generate exactly the type of individual consuming subject required by capitalism. Yet at the same time it appears a wasted production and a failure to invest'. The combination of masturbation and contemporary pornography is best understood through Preciado's (2013) articulation of the post-Second World War era as pharmacopornographic. In the time of birth control pills and sperm banks that separate heterosex from bio-reproduction, masturbating attains a productive as well as consumerist value. The pornographic industry and the industry of masturbation is pharmacopornographic production. Porno-masturbation becomes neither a waste nor a perversion. By linking an everyday sexual act with image-based consumption, masturbation becomes a capitalist act of excessive production and opens cum up to having a utility beyond bio-reproduction. These other utilities, of which the cumshot is one, are not a wasting of cum, but a regulation and maintenance of it towards various ideologies of power and normativity operating at cellular (spermatozoic and telecommunication) levels.

We can also consider the cumshot as a neoliberal expression that conflates work and pleasure, the public and domestic. Neoliberalism's demand for the collapse of work and leisure, the demand for belief and surveillance of productivity is well suited to the cumshot. Further the cumshot succeeds because of the neoliberal work it does in streamlining colonial production by reducing the number of steps necessary for its operation. The cumshot collapses labour and product, the body of the labourer is also the site of production. Blood, sweat and tears are by-products of labour, only cum is produced by bodily labour *and* the intended material of that labour. Only cum can occupy the two dominant colonial definitions of property – Locke's definition of property as labour, and Blackstone's (1979) definition of property as that which can be inherited. Only cum is both a fluid neoliberal signifier, and a rigid, violent white supremacist bio-reproductive material. As a fluid, cum's meaning is free to change without recognition of that change, or as Aydemir (2007) argues, it is productive of masculinity because of its very ambivalence. Its contradictory reception as a natural, normal, male substance and as a shifting signifier is produced by 'a disavowal of historical specificity, a disavowal that occupies normalcy as something that is as it always was and will always be' (Jagose 2013, pp. 67–8). Cum is a floating signifier that benefits from its slippery, abstract materiality while being underpinned by an assumed definitive, gendered, bio-reproductive agency. This particular neocolonial cum does not exist outside the cumshot and while separate (as material and image) they are constitutive elements of each other and have to be thought together.

The cumshot is neocolonial, there were no cumshots before neocolonisation, however the contemporary settler is both colonial and neocolonial. His cum/cumming as and with the cumshot is Lockean and material but only because of new neoliberal and neocolonial structures of property and work. His cum is bio-reproductive, the literal substance of white colonial futurity, but it is also excessive and abstract. It is social, mediated and distributed, but it is also a substance that distinctly marks his property as his own – property that he and the state violently defend. Colonial cum's continuing contradictory daily production by settlers should not mean we label it as ineffective, but rather recognise it as a composition that is endemic to, and productive of, the complex machinations of contemporary settler occupation.

Decolonising the cumshot

The co-dependent emergence of settler sexuality and modern pornography, with the latter providing the image library and archive for the former, means that colonisation is the structuring principle of pornography. The cumshot may be shared beyond white male bodies, even into spaces of conditional sovereignty, yet these new relations are still mapped towards a nation state, international law and capitalism which limits decolonial futures. The reconfiguration of the cumshot does not undo its inherent nationalism. Only the erasure of the cumshot, the removal of it from representation would begin to decolonise sex in ways that address the move towards repatriation of Indigenous land. To erase the cumshot requires the destruction of the whole regime of pornographic imagery. However, as this book claims, pornography is a relational genre, which makes decolonising the cumshot a total project that does not stop at the "boundary" of pornography. Selective censorship is the system we have now, and it works to prevent myriad, diverse and complex Indigenous fantasies from being named, represented and critiqued. To remove the cumshot would necessitate the removal of all other images, and the networks, property and violence that protects them. It would require the banishing of the colonial cum producing subject, whose existence rather than production becomes recognised as excessive. Indigenous peoples' rightful reclamation of cum and its representation wouldn't mean a return to some orgasmic pure jouissance that could finally be enjoyed, nor would it be a slow anti-futurity ultimately leading to settler elimination. What comes next cannot be thought, because decolonisation is total. However, perhaps the Karrabing Film Collective provides a clue. In their film, *Windjarrameru (The Stealing C*nt$)* from 2015, two Karrabing men are chased onto sacred land by police. The police stop at the edge of the sacred land, as though transfixed by an invisible force. What appears at first to be the operation of sacred law, is revealed to be the fear of a toxic waste dump, located on sacred land. The Karrabing men do not stop, but inhabit a land that is both toxic and sacred. As Povinelli (2015) writes '[Indigenous] sovereignty now thrives where Europeans have come, destroyed, and are fearful of returning but to which the Karrabing continue to hold on'. The land and the people existed before, during, outside and within colonisation, and they will exist after it. Erasure is never absolute, a decolonial world will be toxic and sacred. A decolonial world is not mine.

Notes

1 In 1991, at the First International Conference on Orgasm, the sexologist John Money said, 'We use the rule-of-thumb to test that, no matter how they name it, those who are not sure if they've had an orgasm, almost certainly have not had one' (cited in Jagose 2013, p. 72).
2 In still image pornography this distinction can be seen between categories of "cumshot" and "facial", differentiating between ejaculation and semen on a person's face. However, both of these categories describe parts of the sequence of the cumshot.
3 As Lee (2014) summarises, 'ejaculate has long been understood as a sacred symbol of power through procreation and fertility in Western society and science (Moore 2008, Visual AIDS 1999, Schilder *et al.* 2008)'. Even traditions such as throwing rice over the bride at weddings is a symbolic gesture of throwing semen. Taken out of the context of a wedding ceremony it has a lot in common with the gesture of the contemporary cumshot.
4 In Ziplow's (1977, p. 34) manual he warns that porn producers should 'plan on at least ten separate cum shots'. Delacroix, a contemporary porn producer, talks the time pressures of time on set, with small profit margins meaning they cannot wait for a cum shot. With six "orgasms" per scene required, the necessity to fake it is part of the production process (Hay 2016).

5 Ziplow (1977, p. 86) writes of the practicalities of faking the cumshot 'you can put some inserts in later on – just use footage of someone else when you need penetration shots. Try to use a penis that looks like your actor's'. He goes on to provide different recipes for fake cum: 'always bring along a can of concentrated milk ... use it straight or add a small quantity of corn starch which thickens the mixture and gives it a better taste'.

6 Aydemir and Tuck are characterising Williams in these quotes. While Williams does tend towards conflation of orgasm and ejaculation, her reading of the cumshot is more focused on the audience's interpretation of it. As such these quotes are indicative of the general understanding of the cumshot in pornography.

7 This can be evidenced by the heat maps that videos on *Pornhub* feature. In almost every instance of heteroporn the spike in the heat map timeline indicates the cumshot. This demonstrates that videos are being watched disjointedly and that the cumshot is signalled to the audience as an easily identifiable and navigable point.

8 The reference to garbled norms is taken from Berlant and Warner (1998, p. 548) who, in describing heteronormativity, state it is constituted by 'garbled but powerful norms supporting that privilege'.

9 The final version of the Commission has been lost, and only a draft remains. In the draft the quoted section has been crossed out. It is not known if this section was in the final version.

10 This aspect of masturbation appears in Derrida's articulation of the supplement. Derrida uses masturbation as an example of substitution where it is argued as 'originary' (1998, p. 156). The double interpretation of the supplement's purpose (in excess and as lacking) is useful for thinking through masturbation's apparent ambiguity in theory and practice. In addition, thinking of masturbation as originary, always already composed of representations (Derrida 1998, p. 156), places pornography/masturbation as coming before and/or always being present in all sexual expressions. In this sense we can understand pornography as producing settler sexuality through masturbation.

11 Berlant and Warner's (1998, p. 555) "sex act" is presumably coupled heterosex and not masturbation. As they state, 'the sex act shielded by the zone of privacy is the affectional nimbus that heterosexual culture protects and from which it abstracts its model of ethics'. This affectional nimbus is potentially a fiction of heterosexual culture itself.

12 This focus on "truths" that are understood as located in bodies different to the audience is a focus and concern for Williams who states, 'if pornography is a genre that seeks to confess the discursive truths of sex, then what happens when racialized bodies are asked to reveal their particular "truths"?' (Williams 2004, p. 8).

13 It is important here to note that "sex between men" through the cumshot is always mediated and with an abstracted fraternity of white penises. Friendship studies has provided queer pathways by defining homosociality (in part by de-emphasising sex) through 'family' (Budgeon and Roseneil 2002), 'kinship' (Butler 2002), 'friendship' (Foucault 1997, Bray 2003, Derrida 1998, Bell and Binnie 2000), 'public' (Berlant and Warner 1998). For a comprehensive history of queer friendship see Stamp (2009).

The centrality of homosociality to normativity is its radical potential, however the cumshot does not offer opportunities for friendship, only for solidarity and fraternity – a brotherhood of white men, a nation of white men, whose power is in their representative similarity, not their shared aisthesis. This is particularly relevant to Australia where masturbating white fraternity is opposed to Aboriginal brothers/cousins/kin. In the former genealogy is a racial determination confirming their proper place in politics, in the latter genealogy is a general confusion as to relations and incest taboos that mark Indigenous people as ignorant of, or perverted within modern sexuality.

14 As Petersen (1994, p. 67) states, 'What makes ejaculating on the outside degrading ... while ejaculating inside ... sacred? ... masturbating guys ejaculate on their own bodies all the time and not one says Oh God, I just degraded myself'.

15 This community is imagined as it cannot be seen while watching porn, however it is also precisely quantified as most porn videos have a counter of how many people have viewed it. The community of white penises is more direct on sites such as *Chaturbate* where live cam sex is streamed to an audience who are encouraged to interact with the actors and other viewers.

16 'Location of experience' is bell hooks' (1996) description of whiteness. It can be applied to the settler's cum that through orgasm and material locates his experience as protected within private property.

17 As Moore (2007, p. 5) states 'orgasm is conflated with ejaculation, even though one can occur without the other'.

18 Jagose (2013, pp. 194–5) does acknowledge men can also fake orgasms, however the alterity of fake orgasm is specific to women.

19 This distinction between work and labour borrows from Hannah Arendt (2013). I use it more in the simplistic sense than colonial powers and Locke does to make natural claims to occupation and property, while also excluding Indigenous people from making similar natural claims.

20 As Curthoys (1999, pp. 2–3) states 'Australian popular historical mythology stresses struggle, courage and survival, amidst pain, tragedy and loss ... a history of suffering, sacrifice and defiance in defeat'. Similarly Moreton-Robinson (2015, p. 29) notes 'the literature on colonial Britishness expressed through the bush battler, the pioneer, the explorer, and the convict place these founding ancestors as struggling against the landscape', she goes on to specifically address the flattening of Indigenous people, 'it is the landscape that must be conquered, claimed, and named, not Indigenous people, who at the level of the subconscious are perceived to be part of the landscape and thus not human'.

21 The argument for the connection between bodily fluids and property claims can be found in antislavery and independence movements (O'Brein 2013). Bodily fluids have also been used for property claims in early Indigenous land rights arguments, Bloom (2002, p. 501) quotes the *Cherokee Advocate* from 1889;

> In the sense that one man has as much right as another to get a decent and happy living for himself and family by the sweat of his brow, and in that sense and no other, is the land of the Cherokee Nation

common property. Keeping that fact constantly in view, a man's home, a man's improvements, a man's property of all descriptions are as inviolably his, and as rigidly secured to him by the laws of this nation, as the same kind of property is to anybody else in the world, under any other government.

22 For Locke, because women are a passive, natural resource they could not own property. As Folbre (2009, p. 25) writes of Locke, 'only men made choices and responded to incentives' and hence were eligible for natural rights – women only had natural obligations. This ideology structures masturbation, as it is the man who responds to incentives and chooses to actively masturbate. Female masturbation is not considered deliberate or aware and hence have no colonial value.

Bibliography

Ahmed, Sara 2006, *Queer phenomenology: Orientations, objects, others*, Duke University Press, Durham, NC.
Aja, dir. 1991, *Outback Assignment*, Australia.
Altman, Jon and Susie Russell 2012, 'Too much "dreaming": Evaluations of the Northern Territory National Emergency Response Intervention 2007–2012', *Evidence Base Journal*, vol. 3, pp. 1–24.
Anderson, Perry 1961, 'Portugal and the End of Ultra-colonialism', *New Left Review*, vol. 15, 16, 17, pp. 82–102, 88–123, 85–114.
anon. dir. 1999, *Victoria Blue*, Australia.
Arendt, Hannah 2013, *The Human Condition*, University of Chicago Press, Chicago, IL.
Asiedu-Akrofi, Derek 1989, 'Judicial recognition and adoption of customary law in Nigeria', *The American Journal of Comparative Law*, vol. 37, no. 3, pp. 571–93.
Australian Bureau of Statistics 2003, '2017.0 – Census of Population and Housing: Selected Education and Labour Force Characteristics, 2001', viewed 12 July 2019, www.abs.gov.au/ausstats/abs@.nsf/7d12b0f6763c78 caca257061001cc588/60228e033c5ef4f1ca256d010081a7f0!Open Document.
Aydemir, Murat 2007, *Images of Bliss: Ejaculation, Masculinity, Meaning*, University of Minnesota Press, Minneapolis, MN.
Balce, Nerissa S 2006, 'The Filipina's Breast: SAVAGERY, DOCILITY, AND THE EROTICS OF THE AMERICAN EMPIRE', *Social Text*, vol. 24, no. 2, pp. 89–110.
Barthes, Roland 1990, *The Fashion System*, trans. Matthew Ward and Richard Howard, University of California Press, Berkley, CA.
Bataille, Georges 1962, *Erotism*, City Lights Books, San Francisco, CA.
Batchen, Geoffrey 2008, 'Snapshots: Art history and the ethnographic turn', *Photographies*, vol. 1, no. 2, pp. 121–42.
Baudrillard, Jean 2003, *Passwords*, Verso, Brooklyn, NY.
Bell, David and Jon Binnie 2000, *The sexual citizen: Queer politics and beyond*, Polity, Cambridge.

Bennett, Jill 2012, *Practical aesthetics: Events, affect and art after 9/11*, I.B. Tauris, London.
Berger, John 2008, *Ways of seeing. Vol. 1*, Penguin, London.
Berlant, Lauren 2009, 'Two Girls, Fat and Thin', in eds Diane P Herndl and Robyn Warhol-Down, *Feminisms Redux: An Anthology of Literary Theory and Criticism*, Rutgers University Press, New Brunswick, NJ.
Berlant, Lauren ed. 2000, *Intimacy*, University of Chicago Press, Chicago, IL.
Berlant, Lauren and Michael Warner 1998, 'Sex in public', *Critical inquiry*, vol. 24, no. 2, pp. 547–66.
Bersani, Leo 2009, *Homos*, Harvard University Press, Cambridge, MA.
Blackstone, William 1979, *Commentaries on the Laws of England. Volume 1*, University of Chicago Press, Chicago, IL.
Bloom, Khaled J 2002, 'An American tragedy of the Commons: Land and labor in the Cherokee nation, 1870–1900', *Agricultural history*, vol. 76, no. 3, pp. 497–523.
Bone, John T. dir. 1991, *Lost in Paradise*, Australia.
Bray, Alan 2003, *The Friend*, Chicago University Press, Chicago, IL.
Brooks, Peter 1992, *Reading for the Plot: Design and Intention in Narrative*, Harvard University Press, Cambridge, MA.
Buckley, Vincent 1983, *Cutting Green Hay: Friendships, movements and cultural conflicts in Australia's great decades*, Penguin, Melbourne.
Budgeon, Shelley and Sasha Roseneil 2002, 'Cultures of intimacy and care beyond 'the family': Friendship and sexual/love relationships in the twenty-first century', *International Sociological Association World Congress of Sociology*, July, Brisbane, Australia, pp. 8–13.
Butler, Judith 2013, 'Endangered/Endangering: Schematic Racism and White Paranoia', in ed. Robert Gooding-Williams, *Reading Rodney King/reading urban uprising*, Routledge, London.
Butler, Judith 2002, 'Is kinship always already heterosexual?' *differences: A Journal of Feminist Cultural Studies*, vol. 13, no. 1, pp. 14–44.
Byrd, Jodi A 2011, *The transit of empire: Indigenous critiques of colonialism*, University of Minnesota Press, Minneapolis, MN.
Chun, Wendy Hui Kyong and Sarah Friedland 2015, 'Habits of leaking: Of sluts and network cards', *differences*, vol. 26, no. 2, pp. 1–28.
Clark, Kenneth 1972, *The Nude: A Study in Ideal Form*, Princeton University Press, Princeton, NJ.
Clark, Maddee 2016, 'Coded Devices', *Worn Hole*, 6 April, viewed 14 October 2019, http://2016.nextwave.org.au/essays/coded-devices/.
Clark, Manning 1963, *A Short History of Australia*, Penguin, UK.
Clemens, Justin and Dominic Pettman 2010, *Avoiding the subject: Media, culture and the object*, Amsterdam University Press, Amsterdam.
Coulthard, Glen S 2018, 'Introduction', in Manuel, George and Michael Posluns, *The fourth world: An Indian reality*, University of Minnesota Press, Minneapolis, MN.

Crawford, Robert 2010, 'Learning to Say G'day to the World: The Development of Australia's Marketable Image in the 1980s', *Consumption, Markets and Culture*, vol. 13, no. 1, pp. 43–59.

Curthoys, Ann 1999, 'Expulsion, Exodus, and Exile, Imaginary Homelands', *Journal of Australian Studies*, vol. 23, no. 61, pp. 1–19.

Darby, Robert 2005, *A surgical temptation: The demonization of the foreskin and the rise of circumcision in Britain*, University of Chicago Press, Chicago, IL.

Davis, Melody D 1991, *The male nude in contemporary photography*, Temple University Press, Philadelphia, PA.

Davis, Megan and Steve Larkin 2011, *Northern Territory Emergency Response Evaluation Report* (Cwlth), Canberra.

Debord, Guy 2014, *Society of the Spectacle*, trans. Knabb, Ken, Bureau of Public Secrets, Louisiana, LA.

Deloria, Joseph P 1998, *Playing Indian*, Yale University Press, New Haven, CT.

Denoon, Donald 1979, 'Understanding Settler Societies', *Historical Studies*, vol. 18, pp. 511–27.

Derrida, Jacques 1998, *Of Grammatology*, Johns Hopkins University Press, Baltimore, MD.

Derrida, Jacques 1988, 'The politics of friendship', *The Journal of Philosophy*, vol. 85, no. 11, pp. 632–44.

Donzelot, Jacques 1979, *The policing of families*, trans. Hurley, Robert, Pantheon Books, New York, NY.

Duncombe, Jean and Dennis Marsden 1993, 'Love and Intimacy: The Gender Division of Emotion and Emotion Work, A Neglected Aspect of Sociological Discussion of Heterosexual Relationships', *Sociology*, vol. 27, no. 2, pp. 221–41.

Duran, Jane 2009, 'Education and Feminist Aesthetics: Gauguin and the Exotic', *The Journal of Aesthetic Education*, vol. 43, no. 4, pp. 88–95.

Dworkin, Andrea 1995, 'Speech, Equality and Harm: Feminist Legal Perspectives on Pornography and Hate Propaganda', in eds Laura Lederer and Richard Delgado, *The Price We Pay: The Case Against Racist Speech, Hate Propaganda, and Pornography*, Hill and Wang, New York, NY.

Edelman, Lee 2004, *No future: queer theory and the death drive*, Duke University Press, Durham, NC.

Faiman, Peter dir. 1986, *Crocodile Dundee*, Australia.

Faludi, Susan 1995, 'The Money Shot', *The New Yorker*, 30 October, pp. 65–70.

Ferro, Marc 1997, *Colonization: A Global History*, Routledge, London.

Flynn, Michelle dir. 2015, *Momentum Vol 1–4*, Australia.

Foucault, Michel 2007, *Security, Territory, Population: Lectures at the Collège de France 1977–1978*, ed. Michel Senellart, trans. Burchell, Graham, Palgrave Macmillan, UK.

Foucault, Michel 1997, 'Friendship as a way of life', *Ethics: Subjectivity and Truth. Essential Works of Foucault 1954–1984, Volume 1*, ed. Paul Rabinow, Penguin, London, pp. 135–40.

Foucault, Michel 1984, *Résumé des cours 1970–1982*, Jilliard, Paris.

Foucault, Michel 1978, *The History of Sexuality. Vol. 1, An Introduction*, trans. Robert Hurley, Pantheon, New York, NY.

Folbre, Nancy 2009, *Greed, Lust & Gender: A History of Economic Ideas*, Oxford University Press, Oxford.

Garlick, Steve 2012, 'Masculinity, pornography, and the history of masturbation', *Sexuality & Culture*, vol. 16, no. 3, pp. 306–20.

Geczy, Adam 2014, 'Straight Internet Porn and the Natrificial: Body and Dress', *Fashion Theory*, vol. 18, no. 2, pp. 169–87.

Gilman, Sander L 1985, *Difference and Pathology: Stereotypes of Sexuality, Race, and Madness*, Cornell University Press, Ithaca, NY.

Gould, Marty 2011, *Nineteenth-century Theatre and the Imperial Encounter*, Routledge, Abingdon.

Gregory, Tim 2017, 'The maintenance of white heteronormativity in porn films that use Australia as an exotic location', *Porn Studies*, vol. 4, no. 1, pp. 88–104.

Gregory, Tim and Astrid Lorange 2018, 'Teaching post-pornography', *Cultural Studies Review*, vol. 24, no. 1, pp. 137–49.

Hage, Ghassan 1998, *White Nation: Fantasies of White Supremacy in a Multicultural Society*, Pluto Press Australia, Sydney.

Hallam, Paul 2004, 'If you look at it long enough …' *Journal of homosexuality*, vol. 47, no. 3–4, pp. 59–74.

Halperin, David M 1994, 'Historicizing the subject of desire: Sexual preferences and erotic identities in the Pseudo-Lucianic Erotes', in ed. Goldstein Jan E, *Foucault and the Writing of History*, Blackwell, Hoboken, NJ.

Hansen, Christian, Catherine Needham and Bill Nichols, 1991, 'Pornography, ethnography, and the discourses of power', in ed. Bill Nichols, *Representing Reality: Issues and Concepts in Documentary*, Indiana University Press, Indianapolis.

Harris, Cheryl I 1992, 'Whiteness as property', *Harvard Law Review*, vol. 106, no. 8, pp. 1710–91.

Hay, Mark 2016, 'The Oral History of the Money Shot', *Vice*, 12 December, viewed 15 November 2018, www.vice.com/en_us/article/qkbwd5/an-oral-history-of-the-moneyshot.

hooks, bell 1996, *Killing rage: Ending racism*, Penguin, London.

Hughes, Robert 1987, *The Fatal Shore: A History of Transportation of Convicts to Australia, 1797–1868*, Collins Harville, London.

Jagose, Annamarie 2013, *Orgasmology*, Duke University Press, Durham, NC.

Jameson, Fredric 2013, *Signatures of the Visible*, Routledge, London.

Johnson, Eithne 1993, 'Excess and Ecstasy: Constructing Female Pleasure in Porn Movies', *The Velvet Light Trap*, vol. 32, pp. 30–50.

Joone, dir. 2005, *Pirates*, Adam & Eve Pictures and Digital Playground, USA.

Jordan, Glenn and Chris Weedon 1995, *Cultural Politics: Class, Gender, Race, and the Postmodern World*, Wiley-Blackwell, Hoboken, NJ.

Karskens, Grace 2011, 'The myth of Sydney's foundational orgy', *Dictionary of Sydney*, viewed 2 August 2018, http://dictionaryofsydney.org/entry/the_myth_of_sydneys_foundational_org.

Karskens, Grace 2009, *The colony: a history of early Sydney*, Allen & Unwin, Sydney.

Kelley, Robin D G 2017, 'The rest of us: Rethinking settler and native', *American Quarterly*, vol. 69, no. 2, pp. 267–76.

Khamis, Susie 2012, 'Brand Australia: Half-truths for a Hard Sell', *Journal of Australian Studies*, vol. 36, no. 1, pp. 49–63.

King, Andrew 2005, 'Reconciling Nicci Lane: The "Unspeakable" Significance of Australia's First Indigenous Porn Star 1', *Continuum: Journal of Media & Cultural Studies*, vol. 19, no. 4, pp. 523–43.

Kingwin, Sam 2018, 'Top 20: Native American Pornstars (2019)', *Redbled Dripping Adult Content*, 17 December, viewed 14 June 2019, www.redbled.com/native-american-pornstars/.

Kipnis, Laura 2014, *Bound and gagged: Pornography and the politics of fantasy in America*, Duke University Press, Durham, NC.

Kirsch, Robert, Paul Moris, Cindy Patton, Michael Scarce and Nicolas Sheon, 28 May, *Table Discussion*, viewed 5 July 2019, http://hivinsite.ucsf.edu/InSite?page¼pa-2098-4218.

Korff, Jens 2006, 'Northern Territory Emergency Response (NTER) – "The Intervention"', *Creative Spirits*, viewed 21 March 2016, www.creativespirits.info/aboriginalculture/politics/northern-territory-emergency-response-intervention#ixzz43VGaeqg2.

Landes, Xavier and Morten E J Nielsen 2018, 'Racial dodging in the porn industry: a case with no silver bullet', *Porn Studies*, vol. 5, no. 2, pp. 115–30.

Lee, Byron 2014, 'It's a question of breeding: Visualizing queer masculinity in bareback pornography', *Sexualities*, vol. 12, no. 1/2, pp. 100–20.

Lehamn, Peter 1999, 'Ed Powers and the Fantasy of Documenting Sex', in eds Elias, James, Elias Veronica D, Bullough Vern L, Brewer Gwen, Douglas Jeffery J, Jarvis, Will, *Porn 101: Eroticism, Pornography, and the First Amendment*, Prometheus Books, New York, NY.

Locke, John 2018, *The Works of John Locke, Vol. 2*, Fb&c Limited, London.

Locke, John 2017, *Theoretical and Empirical Studies of Rights*, Routledge, London.

Longford, Lord 1972, *Pornography: The Longford Report*, Coronet, London.

Lukinbeal, Chris 2005, 'Cinematic Landscapes', *Journal of Cultural Geography*, vol. 23, no. 1, pp. 3–22.

Mabo and Others v. Queensland (No. 2) 1992, HCA 23.

McKee, Alan 1999, 'Australian gay porn videos: The national identity of despised cultural objects', *International Journal of Cultural Studies*, vol. 2, no. 2, pp. 178–98.

McKenna, Mark 2000, 'First Words: A Brief History of Public Debate on a New Preamble to the Australian Constitution 1991–99', *Parliament of Australia*, Research Paper 16, Canberra, viewed 12 October 2019, www.aph.gov.au/About_Parliament/Parliamentary_Departments/Parliamentary_Library/pubs/rp/rp9900/2000RP16.

McNair, Brian 2014, 'Rethinking the effects paradigm in porn studies', *Porn Studies*, no. 1–2, pp. 161–71.

Manuel, George and Michael Posluns 2018, *The fourth world: An Indian reality*, University of Minnesota Press, Minneapolis, MN.

Mar, Tracey Banivanua 2016, *Decolonisation and the Pacific: indigenous globalisation and the ends of empire*, Cambridge University Press, Cambridge.

Mawhinney, Janet L 1999, 'Giving up the ghost, disrupting the (re) production of white privilege in anti-racist pedagogy and organizational change', PhD diss., *Bibliothèque nationale du Canada*, Ottawa.

Metherell, Mark 2006, 'No thank you, greets Abbott's call for new paternalism', *Sydney Morning Herald*, 22 June, viewed 23 July 2019, www.smh.com.au/national/no-thank-you-greets-abbotts-call-for-new-paternalism-20060622-gdnt32.html.

Mignolo, Walter 2011, *The darker side of western modernity: Global futures, decolonial options*, Duke University Press, Durham, NC.

Mitropoulos, Angela 2012, *Contract & Contagion: from biopolitics to oikonomia*, Minor Compositions, New York, NY.

Moore, Lisa J 2008, *Sperm counts: Overcome by man's most precious fluid*, New York University Press, New York, NY.

Moreton-Robinson, Aileen 2018, 'Bodies That Matter on the Beach', *E-flux*, vol. 90, April.

Moreton-Robinson, Aileen 2015, *The white possessive: Property, power, and indigenous sovereignty*, University of Minnesota Press, Minneapolis, MN.

Moreton-Robinson, Aileen 2005, 'The house that Jack built: Britishness and white possession', *Australian Critical Race and Whiteness Studies Association eJournal*, vol. 1, pp. 21–9.

Morgan, Jonathan dir. 2008, *The Cougar Hunter*, USA.

Morgensen, Scott L 2011, *Spaces between us: Queer settler colonialism and indigenous decolonization*, University of Minnesota Press, Minneapolis, MN.

Morris, Paul, and Susanna Paasonen 2014, 'Risk and Utopia A Dialogue on Pornography', *GLQ: A journal of Lesbian and Gay Studies*, vol. 20, no. 3, pp. 215–39.

Moten, Fred 2015, 'Blackness and Nonperformance', *The Museum of Modern Art*, 25 September, viewed 23 July 2019, www.youtube.com/watch?v=G2leiFByIIg.

Mulholland, Monique 2016, ' "The pathological native" versus "the good white girl": an analysis of race and colonialism in two Australian porn panics', *Porn Studies*, vol. 3, no. 1, pp. 34–49.

Nash, Jennifer C 2014, *The black body in ecstasy: Reading race, reading pornography*, Duke University Press, Durham, NC.

Nead, Lynda 2002, *The female nude: Art, obscenity and sexuality*, Routledge, London.
Nead, Lynda 1990, 'The Female Nude: Pornography, Art, and Sexuality', *Signs*, vol. 15, no. 2, pp. 323–35.
O'Brien, Colleen C 2013, 'Paternal Solicitude and Haitian Emigration: The First American Occupation?', *South Central Review*, no. 30, vol. 1, pp. 32–54.
Paasonen, Susanna 2014, 'Between Meaning and Mattering: On Affect and Porn Studies', *Porn Studies*, vol. 1–2, pp. 136–42.
Paasonen, Susanna 2011, *Carnal resonance: Affect and online pornography*, MIT Press, Cambridge, MA.
Paasonen, Susanna, Kaarina Nikunen and Laura Saarenmaa 2007, *Pornification: sex and sexuality in media culture*, Berg Publishers, Oxford.
Paisley, Fiona 2003, 'White Settler Colonialisms and the Colonial Turn: An Australian Perspective', *Journal of Colonialism and Colonial History*, vol. 4, no. 3.
Papastephanou, Marianna and Zelia Gregoriou 2014, 'Locke's Children? Rousseau and the Beans (Beings?) of the Colonial Learner', *Studies in Philosophy and Education*, vol. 33, no. 5, pp. 463–80.
Patton, Cindy 1989, 'Hegemony and Orgasm – Or the Instability of Heterosexual Pornography', *Screen*, vol. 30, no. 1–2, pp. 100–13.
Pease, Allison 2000, *Modernism, Mass Culture, and the Aesthetics of Obscenity*, Cambridge University Press, Cambridge, MA.
Peterson, James R 1994, 'Forum', *Playboy*, March.
Phillip, Arthur 2010, 'Governor Phillip's instructions 25 April 1787', *Museum of Australian Democracy*, viewed 10 October 2019, www.foundingdocs.gov.au/resources/transcripts/nsw2_doc_1787.pdf.
Pornhub 2018, '2018 Year in Review', *Pornhub Insights*, viewed 2 July 2019, www.pornhub.com/insights/2018-year-in-review.
Povinelli, Elizabeth A 2015, 'Windjarrameru, The Stealing C*nts', *E-Flux Supercommunity*, 21 May, viewed 12 September 2018, http://supercommunity.e-flux.com/texts/windjarrameru-the-stealing-c-nts/.
Povinelli, Elizabeth A 2002, *The cunning of recognition: indigenous alterities and the making of Australian multiculturalism*, Duke University Press, Durham, NC.
Preciado, Paul B 2015, 'Posporn Activism', trans. Smith, Sam, *Parole De Queer*, 27 May, viewed 3 July 2019, http://paroledequeer.blogspot.com/2015/05/postporno-activism-by-paul-b-preciado.html.
Preciado, Paul B 2013, *Testo junkie: Sex, drugs, and biopolitics in the pharmacopornographic era*, The Feminist Press, New York, NY.
Racial Discrimination Act 1975 (Cwlth), viewed 20 June 2019, www.comlaw.gov.au/.
Radcliffe, Sarah A 2017, 'Decolonising geographical knowledges', *Transactions of the Institute of British Geographers*, vol. 42, no. 3, pp. 329–33.
Rancière, Jacques 2010, *Chronicles of Consensual Times*, trans. Corcoran, Steven, Continuum, New York, NY.

Rancière, Jacques 2004, *The Politics of Aesthetics*, trans. Rockhill, Gabriel, Continuum, New York, NY.
Rancière, Jacques 1999, *Disagreement: Politics and philosophy*, trans. Rose, Julie, University of Minnesota Press, Minneapolis, MN.
Rancière, Jacques, Davide Panagia and Rachel Bowlby 2001, 'Ten theses on politics', *Theory & event*, vol. 5, no. 3.
Reynolds, Henry 2003, *The Law of the Land*, Penguin, London.
Reynolds, Michael 2002, *Sunday Special*, Optimystic Research, Paris.
Rosaldo, Renato 1989, 'Imperialist nostalgia', *Representations*, vol. 26, pp. 107–22.
Rose, Gillian 2016, *Doing family photography: The domestic, the public and the politics of sentiment*, Routledge, London.
Said, Edward W 1994, *Orientalism*, Vintage, New York, NY.
Said, Edward W 1993, *Culture and Imperialism*, Vintage, New York, NY.
Schilder, Arn J, Treena R Orchard, Christopher S Buchner, Mary Lou Miller, Kim A Fernandes, Robert S Hogg, and Steffanie A Strathdee 2008, ' "It's like the treasure": beliefs associated with semen among young HIV-positive and HIV-negative gay men', *Culture, Health & Sexuality*, vol. 10, no. 7, pp. 667–79.
Sedgwick, Eve Kosofsky 2015, *Between men: English literature and male homosocial desire*, Columbia University Press, New York, NY.
Senate Community Affairs Legislation Committee, *Families, Housing, Community Services and Indigenous Affairs and Other Legislation Amendment (Restoration of Racial Discrimination Act) Bill 2009* (Cwlth), viewed 15 March 2019, www.aph.gov.au/Parliamentary_Business/Bills_Legislation/Bills_Search_Results/Result?bId=s738.
Shepard, Todd 2006, *The Invention of Decolonization: The Algerian War and the Remaking of France*, Cornell University Press, Ithaca, NY.
Shimizu, Celine P 2007, *The Hypersexuality of Race: Performing Asian/American Women on Screen and Scene*, Duke University Press, Durham, NC.
Silva, Tony 2017, 'Bud-sex: Constructing normative masculinity among rural straight men that have sex with men', *Gender & Society*, vol. 31, no. 1, pp. 51–73.
Slemon, Stephen 1990, 'Unsettling the Empire: Resistance Theory for the Second World', *Journal of Postcolonial Writing*, vol. 30, no. 2, pp. 30–41.
Smith, Jesus G and Aurolyn Luykx 2017, 'Race play in BDSM porn: The eroticization of oppression', *Porn Studies*, vol. 4, no. 4, pp. 433–46.
Smith, Paul 1988, 'Vas', *Camera Obscura*, vol. 17, May, pp. 89–112.
Smyth, Arthur B 1788, 'Journal 1787–1789, compiled c1790', *Mitchell Library*, entry for 6 February 1788, viewed 11 June 2018, http://acms.sl.nsw.gov.au/_transcript/2007/D00007/a1085.html#a1085090.
Solomon-Godeau, Abigail 1986, 'The legs of the countess', *October*, no. 39, pp. 65–108.
Solomon-Godeau, Abigail and Linda Nochlin,1991, *Photography at the Dock: Essays in Photographic History, Institutions, and Practices*, University of Minnesota Press, Minneapolis.

Sontag, Susan 1982, *The pornographic imagination*, Penguin, London.
Spencer, Baldwin and Francis J Gillen 1904, *The Northern Tribes of Central Australia*, Macmillan, London.
Stadler, Jane, and Peta Mitchell 2010, 'Never-Never Land: Affective Landscapes, the Touristic Gaze and Heterotopic Space in Australia', *Studies in Australasian Cinema*, vol. 4, no. 2, pp. 173–87.
Stamp, Richard 2009, 'The torsion of politics and friendship in Derrida, Foucault and Rancière', *Borderlands*, vol. 8, no. 2, pp. 1–27.
Stardust, Zahra 2014, 'Fisting is not permitted': criminal intimacies, queer sexualities and feminist porn in the Australian legal context', *Porn Studies*, vol. 1, no. 3, pp. 242–59.
Stewart, Potter 1964, 'Jacobellis v ohio'. *US Rep* 378, 184.
Stoler, Laura A 2010, *Carnal knowledge and imperial power: Race and the intimate in colonial rule*, University of California Press, Berkley, CA.
Stoler, Laura A 1995, *Race and the education of desire: Foucault's history of sexuality and the colonial order of things*, Duke University Press, Durham, NC.
Stratford, Elaine, and Colin Langridge 2012, 'Critical Artistic Interventions into the Geopolitical Spaces of Islands', *Social & Cultural Geography*, vol. 13, no. 7, pp. 821–43.
Stronger Futures in the Northern Territory Act 2012 (Cwlth), viewed 3 April 2019, www.legislation.gov.au/Details/C2012A00100.
Theroux, Paul 1986, *Sunrise with Seamonsters*, Houghton Mifflin Harcourt, Boston, MA.
Tuck, Eve and Wayne K Yang 2012, 'Decolonization is not a metaphor', *Decolonization: Indigeneity, education & society*, vol. 1, no. 1, pp. 1–40.
Tuck, Greg 2009, 'The mainstreaming of masturbation: Autoeroticism and consumer capitalism', in ed. Attwood, Feona, *Mainstreaming sex: The sexualization of Western culture*, I.B. Tauris, London.
Tuck, Greg 2003, 'Mainstreaming the Money Shot: Reflections on the Representation of Ejaculation in Contemporary American Cinema', *Paragraph*, vol. 26, no. 1/2, pp. 263–79.
United Nations General Assembly 2007, *United Nations declaration on the rights of indigenous peoples*, UN General Assembly, New York, NY.
US Attorney General's Commission on Pornography 1986, *Final Report*, Washington, DC.
Veracini, Lorenzo 2013, '"Settler colonialism": Career of a concept', *The Journal of Imperial and Commonwealth History*, vol. 41, no. 2, pp. 313–33.
Visual AIDS 1999, 'Visual AIDS: Gay male porn and safer sex pedagogy', *HIV InSite Round*.
Ward, Jane 2015, *Not gay: Sex between straight white men*, New York University Press, New York, NY.
Ward, Russel B 1978, *The Australian Legend*, Oxford University Press, Oxford.
Warner, Michael ed. 1993, *Fear of a queer planet: Queer politics and social theory*, Vol. 6, University of Minnesota Press, Minneapolis, MN.

Waugh, Thomas 1996, *Hard to imagine: Gay male eroticism in photography and film from their beginnings to Stonewall*, Columbia University Press, New York, NY.

Weber, Max 2003, *The Protestant Ethic and the Spirit of Capitalism*, trans. Parsons, Talcott, Dover Publications, Mineola, NY.

Whitten, Norman and Rachel Corr 2001, 'Contesting The Images Of Oppression: Indigenous Views of Blackness in the Americas', *NACLA Report on the Americas*, vol. 34, no. 6, pp. 24–8.

Wild, Rex and Patricia Anderson 2007, 'Northern Territory Board of Inquiry into the Protection of Aboriginal Children from Sexual Abuse, Ampe Akelyernemane Meke Mekarle: 'Little Children are Sacred': Report of the Northern Territory Board of Inquiry Into the Protection of Aboriginal Children from Sexual Abuse 2007', *Department of the Chief Minister*, Darwin.

Williams, Linda 2014, 'Pornography, porno, porn: Thoughts on a weedy field', *Porn Studies*, no. 1–2, pp. 24–40.

Williams, Linda ed. 2004, *Porn Studies*, Duke University Press, Durham, NC.

Williams, Linda 1999, *Hardcore: Power, pleasure and the 'frenzy of the visible'*, University of California Press, Berkley, CA.

Wolfe, Patrick 2016, *Traces of History: Elementary Structures of Race*, Verso, London.

Wolfe, Patrick 2006, 'Settler Colonialism and the Elimination of the Native', *Journal of genocide research*, vol. 8, no. 4, pp. 387–409.

Wolfe, Patrick 1999, *Settler Colonisation and the Transformation of Anthropology: The Politics and Poetics of an Ethnographic Event*, Cassell, London.

Woodman, Pierre dir. 2000, *The Fugitive 2*, Australia.

Ziplow, Steven 1977, *The Film Maker's Guide to Pornography*, Drake Publishing, New York, NY.

Žižek, Slavoj 1992, *Looking awry: An introduction to Jacques Lacan through popular culture*, MIT Press, Cambridge, MA.

Index

Aboriginal people 35, 48, 51, 69–74; absence of 34, 69, 71; absence of in pornoexotic films 34; breaking cultural, kinship and physical connection to their land 73; character 69–71; communities 18, 57, 71–2; and land rights 57; and the The Northern Territory National Emergency Response (referred to as The Intervention) 57, 71–3; and pornography 68–9; pornstars and settler violence 68; representations of 36, 71
actors 19, 22, 34, 37–40, 54, 59, 64–6, 68–9, 80–1, 87, 91, 95; non-Aboriginal 69, 71; white male 87
African Americans 17, 59–60
agency 6–7, 18, 35, 49, 53, 67; bio-reproductive 98; sexual 18, 25, 50–1, 56, 58; silencing Indigenous and decolonial praxis 18
alterity 59, 90, 95; radical 22, 54, 57, 62; and settler colonies 56
Altman, Jon 71–2
Anderson, Perry 6, 14, 72
animals 31, 38–9
anthropologists 55–6
anthropology 54–5, 57
anti-porn feminist critiques of heteroporn 78
art history 12, 26–7
audiences 22, 26–31, 33, 35, 37–8, 43, 51, 54, 76, 82, 86, 91; domestic 32–3; global 32–3; ignorant 26; international 24, 32; local 32, 76; non-Native 67; white Australian 32
Australia 6, 8, 13, 15, 18, 25, 30–4, 36, 38–42, 44, 46–50, 57, 69–72, 74, 84; colonial narrative 45; colonisation of 33, 45; contemporary 31; environment of 34, 37; gay porn films 33; Government of 72; heteroporn projects 24–5, 50, 69; High Court decisions 57; identity 44–5, 49; and the Lara Bingle campaign 36; and the law concerning pornographic material 73; and local audiences 32; models and media personalities 35; and non-porn films 37; pornoexotic (the exoticisation of heterosex) 24, 31–7, 43–4, 49, 70; pornographic industry 32; and white audiences 32
Australian National Film and Sound Archive 85
authenticity 20, 38, 47–8, 58, 66, 78, 83, 88, 92; conveying 82; eroticising 66; repressive 16
autonomy 94
Aydemir, Murat 19, 21, 82–3, 85, 87, 95, 97

back-page legislation 8
Balce, Nerissa 55
banning pornography 18, 71–4
Berlant, Lauren 49, 88
Bersani, Leo 96
Bingle, Lara 35–6

bio-reproductive coupling 17, 94, 97
biopower 19, 95–6
Black audiences 54, 60
Black Body in Ecstasy 54
Black female bodies 54
Black feminisms 54, 59–60
Blackness (depictions of) 17, 51, 59–61, 68
blood 21, 91–4, 97; relations 43; settler's 79
bodies 2–3, 5–6, 10–11, 16–18, 20–1, 24, 26, 28, 35, 37, 61, 63–4, 85, 92–3, 96–7; Black and brown 6, 55, 59; brown 6; male 20–2, 81, 98; naked 27; non-Native 67; non-white 5, 17, 27; post-pornographic 18, 65; racialised 54; settler's 42, 67, 93–4; white 27–9, 31, 33, 35, 37, 40, 50, 85, 91
Bone, John T. 25

cameras 10, 12, 19, 35, 38–40, 50, 81, 85
campaigns 34–6
capitalism 5, 97–8
Cassidy, Zaya 65–6
Caucasian ethnicity 65
censoring pornography by restricting access 5
censorship 2, 5, 8, 53, 72, 74–6
censorship offences 73
Cherokee 65, 75
child sexual abuse 57, 72–3, 92, 96
children 21, 47, 72, 96
Christian missions 40
claims 7, 16, 19, 45, 48, 61, 66–7, 72–3, 78, 84–5, 93–4, 96; central 48, 95; false 57; indexical 83; natural 84
Clark, Kenneth 1, 12, 47, 56
cocks 64–5
colonial 16, 19, 21, 24, 27, 30, 55, 61–2, 74, 79, 84–5, 90, 92, 94–5, 98–9; art 70, 91; blood 92; children 92; citizenship 57; contact 2, 15, 65, 70; cumshots 78–99; futurity in Australia 48; heteropatriarchy 11; heteroporn 33; heterosexual culture 84; identity 44; labour 21, 37, 46, 48, 91–2; law 48, 53; pornoexotica 18, 31–2, 34, 48–50; pornographic exotica 24–51; projects 62, 79; representational systems 56; violence 2, 24, 48, 75; weapons 56; white expansion 14, 29
colonial structures 15, 61–2, 79; developing 56; transnational 15
colonialism 3, 15–16, 26, 84, 92
colonies 16–17, 21, 25, 31, 42, 44, 47, 61–2; settler 7–8, 13–16, 18, 20–1, 24–5, 41, 43–4, 46–9, 54, 56, 59–60, 62, 84–5, 88–9, 91–2
colonisation 2, 14–15, 17–18, 20–2, 24–5, 27–8, 30, 35–7, 54, 56, 60–1, 83, 91, 93–6, 98–9; abstracts 61; public images of 93; and the requirement to make categories of Native, slave and settler incompatible 58; settler 13, 15, 19, 22, 56, 73–4, 83, 92
colonisers 15, 24, 28, 35, 48, 67; and colonisation 36; and films 38; white 14
colonists 16, 59–60, 62
colour (people) 6, 12, 26–7, 51, 65
community 25, 31, 42–3, 49, 72–3, 84; imagined 19, 88; *Lost in Paradise* 43; polyamorous 38; settler 43; of white masturbators 87
consumption 18, 21, 42, 84, 90, 94; cultural 18; image-based 97; masturbation 97
convicts 42, 47
Corr, Rachel 63
coupled heterosex 19–20, 46, 86, 88–9
coupling, bio-reproductive 17, 94, 97
Crocodile Dundee 34
crocodiles 34, 49
culture 15, 31, 43, 55, 57–8, 61, 67, 83–4, 94; Eastern 26; heterosexual 84, 86; Indigenous 53; Native 67; practices 24, 35, 71, 90; settler 67; sexual 68; visual 18; and Western bodies 31; white nationalist 14

Index

cums 50, 87, 94; *see also* cumshots
cumshots 18–22, 74, 78–99;
    indexical deception 82;
    masturbatory 94; neocolonial 95;
    positions 79; sequence 80–1
curiosity 26, 63; analytical 3–4, 22;
    generation of 25

dangers of pornography 5, 18, 26–7
Darby, Robert 96
Davis, Megan 6, 73
debauchery 48
Debord, Guy 10
decolonial acts 14, 58
decolonial futures 14, 98
decolonial studies 22
decolonialism 14
decolonization 14, 18, 58, 98–9
depravity 26–7, 29
Derrida, Jacques 87
desexualising 67
discourses 14, 46, 57, 59, 72, 96;
    global 95–6; pornographising
    decolonial 22; public 12–13
disembodied penises 80
DNA 66
documentaries 12, 63, 81, 84, 89;
    see also films
Down on his Luck 69
Duncombe, Jean 89
duty 22, 44; bio-reproductive 94;
    and sex 43–4
DVDs 69

early settlements 46–7
Eastern culture 26
economy 14, 16, 22, 60, 85;
    profitable exploitative 14; settler-
    colonial 16, 60; white-dominated
    representational 85
ecstasy 54, 59
egalitarianism 42, 45–6
ejaculating 19, 21–2, 81, 83, 85,
    87–8, 90–1, 95
Eldeman, Lee 19
elimination 2, 16, 24, 61, 64–7;
    assumed 62; ideology of 59–60;
    strategy 72
'elimination logic' 16–17, 64
erotic 27, 31, 67, 86, 90; art 28;

dreams 70; fiction 65; language
    66; value 67
erotica 26, 28, 35, 41, 63, 66, 80
ethnicities 64–7
ethno-pornography 55
ethnographers 53, 61
ethnopornography 53–7, 61, 63, 65,
    67, 75; early twentieth century 54;
    influence of 55
evidence 20, 47, 59, 73, 78–80,
    83–4, 86, 91, 93–4; of behaviour
    change 73; documentary 93; and
    productivity 79
exotic 25–6, 29–35, 37–41, 43,
    50–1, 69–70; erotica 25; fiction
    25; landscapes 35, 37–8; locations
    31, 41; representations 25, 50;
    symbols 28, 39
exotica 28, 31, 40–1
exoticisation 24, 27, 41

fake films 36
fake orgasms 22, 41, 82–3, 90, 95
Faludi, Susan 82
family 4–5, 12, 40, 42, 46, 72, 88,
    91; normative 5; nuclear 5, 45;
    photographs 11–12
family home 5, 97
fantasies 2, 4, 6, 25–7, 29, 31–2,
    37–8, 48–50, 66, 70–2; cinematic
    29; domestic 12; erotic 70;
    masturbatory 55; racial
    pornographic 53; settler's 2, 53;
    sexual 17
fantasy pornoexotic films 30
fear 1, 4–5, 30, 33, 54, 56–7, 74–5,
    96–7, 99; additive 61; of porn for
    the masses 4; unfounded 26
female nudity 55
female orgasm 22, 82, 90
feminism 11
filmic narratives 29–30, 49
films 1, 7, 25, 30, 32, 34, 36–44,
    49–51, 54, 65–6, 69–71, 81, 89,
    99; Australian feature heteroporn
    69; colonial heteroporn 33;
    fantasy pornoexotic 30; foreign
    29; Hollywood 29; micro-budget
    32
Fison, Lorimer 55

Flynn, Michelle 32
foreign films 29
Foucauldian tradition 55, 86
Foucault, Michel 26, 61, 96
framework 15, 17, 59;
    authenticating 84; colonial hetero-
    masculine 44; representational 3
fucking 6–7, 18, 29–30, 37–40,
    50–1, 54, 64–5, 67, 81–2, 84, 88;
    bodies 8, 10, 24, 38; character 38;
    explicit 30; igniting a natural,
    cross-species recognition 39
The Fugitive 2, 12, 25

Garlick, Steve 82, 94
Gauguin, Paul 38, 40
gay 33, 36, 40, 44, 46, 80; identity
    44; policing of 8; porn 33; sex 33
gay pornoexotica 33
Gillen, Francis 55
Gregoriou, Zelia 92

Harris, Cheryl 92
heteronormative porn *see*
    heteroporn
heteronormativity 8, 12, 17, 20, 27,
    33, 43, 46, 62, 89; and
    pornography 10, 17; white 35, 37,
    41, 55
heteroporn 3–4, 9–10, 13, 17, 19,
    28, 31, 49, 53, 65, 67, 78, 80–2,
    84, 86; anti-porn feminist
    critiques of 78; frameworks 74;
    non-Native 64; white 50
heteroporn films 25, 28, 48; *The
    Fugitive* 2, 12, 25; *Lost in
    Paradise* 25; *Outback Assignment*
    25, 39, 41, 69, 71; *Pirates* 29–30;
    Victoria Blue 25, 40–1
heterosex 12, 17, 19–20, 24, 37–9,
    46, 78–80, 83, 86, 89–90, 95; acts
    78, 86; coupled 19–20, 46, 86,
    88–9; explicit 64; partnered 20;
    settler 87; white 37
heterosexual culture 84, 86
heterosexuality 16–17, 20, 44, 46,
    83, 87; monogamous 49; support
    system 89
hierarchies 3, 13, 78; non-
    pornographic 71; normative

representational 8; racial 16, 26;
    sexual 2; white power 46
histories 2–3, 6, 8, 11, 13–14, 16,
    18–19, 21, 30, 35, 54–6, 58–61,
    68, 91, 93; frontier 62; long 14,
    80; parallel 33; porn's 54; visible
    28
Hogan, Paul 34, 36
Hollywood films 29
homoerotica 48–9
homosexuality 33, 44
homosociality 19, 25, 33, 44, 46, 48
hypervisualisation 53–4

icons 32, 93
identity 7, 9, 21, 35–6, 65, 94;
    ethnic 60; national 1; normative
    49; settler's 19
ideologies 4, 59, 84, 97
images 3, 5–6, 8, 10–12, 18, 31, 34,
    65–6, 71, 75, 78, 85–7, 91, 93–5,
    98–9; contrasting 25; domestic 80;
    erasing of 91; framed 87;
    heteronormative 28; iconic 69;
    instrumental 62; new 56, 71;
    singular 80; totemic 80; tourism
    35; tourist 37; visible 72
incompatibility 2, 20, 65, 92;
    imaged 92; racialised 20
independence 13–14, 42; achieving
    national 14; legal 56; legislative
    13
indexicality 6, 78, 83, 86
Indigeneity 8, 16, 21, 51, 55–8, 62,
    64, 66–70, 76
Indigenous 16, 18, 61, 63–5, 68–9,
    76, 85, 99; activists 53;
    appearance in pornography 63;
    Australians in porn 64, 68;
    censoring 51; communities 57;
    culture 53; futurity 2, 20, 54, 58,
    65; land management 92; land
    rights cases 15; pathologising 53;
    pornographic resistance 53;
    pornstars 18
representation 2–3, 17, 67;
    resistance 14; and settler
    independence 13
Indigenous people 2–3, 6, 13–17,
    20, 24–5, 38, 48, 51, 53–76, 85,

91–2, 99; citizenship 57; elimination of 24, 61; exclusion of 54; outside of modern sexuality 61; in porn 54
Indigenous sex 16, 20, 53, 55–7, 61–2, 72; and futurity 61; and sexuality 2, 20, 58, 62
industry 32, 42, 65–6, 97; audiovisual 72; new 19; synthetic 68
infertility 47
Ingre, Jean-Auguste-Dominique 27
innocence 58, 67, 96
Instagram 10
integration 1, 3, 9, 27, 30; garbled 83; total 7
intercourse 55, 86, 89; penial-vaginal 86; vaginal 89
internet 3, 5, 11, 32
Internet Adult Film Database 66
interracial intimacy 71
interracial porn 59–61, 64, 75
The Intervention 57, 71–3
intimacy 38, 49, 71
invisibility 2, 6–7, 9, 50, 53; of Indigenous people 53–4; public 13; total 53

Jacobs, Jennifer 65, 70
Jagose, Annamarie 20, 80, 86, 89–90, 98

kangaroos 39–40
King, Andrew 68–9, 71

labour 14, 20–1, 48, 59, 78–9, 91–5, 97; by-products of 79, 97; colonial 21, 37, 46, 48, 91–2; Locke's definition of 21, 59, 92–3; settler 20–1, 83, 90, 93
Landes, Xavier 59–60
Lane, Nicci 71
Le Bain Turk 27
Lee, Hyapatia 65–6
legacies 14, 57; of biopower and colonisation 95; of ethnopornography 57
Les Demoiselles d'Avignon 27
lesbian sex 8
Little Children are Sacred 6, 72

Locke, John 20–1, 79, 92–3; definition of property 97; understanding of property 79
logic 10, 19, 22, 49, 74–5, 84; capitalist 97; developing culture 3; pioneering 14; racial 26; white possessive 35
Lost in Paradise 25, 37–8, 42–3, 50
Lukinbeal, Chris 35
Luykx, Aurolyn 63

Mabo and Others v. *Queensland (No. 2)* 57
male masturbation 19–20, 82, 86–7, 96–7
male orgasms 78, 81, 86, 88–9
male pleasure 11, 78, 83
male settlers 19–20, 46, 78, 83, 87–8, 93–4, 96; *see also* settlers
Manuel, George 14
masculinity 33, 44–5, 79, 82–3, 87–8, 94–5, 97
masturbating 1, 10, 19–21, 74, 78, 82, 86–8, 90, 94–7; finishing 81; non-Native woman 67; settler 79, 85, 96; viewer 85, 87; woman 67
masturbation 19–20, 28, 79, 82, 84, 86, 88–90, 93–7; *see also* male masturbation
mate-sex 46, 48–9
material production 19–22, 79, 94–5
mateship 25, 33, 36, 44–6, 48–50; activities 49; colonial 49; disguises white power hierarchies in Australia as egalitarianism 46; representations of 46, 48; white masculine 36
Mawhinney, Janet 18, 67
McCubbin, Frederick 69
McKee, Alan 33, 36, 85
media 10–11, 87
Meese Commission 8
micro-budget films 32
Mignolo, Walter 14
miscegenation 16, 21, 56, 62
Mitropoulos, Angela 73
modern sexuality 2, 56–7, 61–3, 65, 67; *see also* sexuality
Modernist paintings 28
Momentum 32

Moreton-Robinson, Aileen 14, 35, 44, 60, 74
Morgan, Lewis 33, 55
Morgensen, Scott 2, 16, 60–1, 67–8
multi-ethnic labelling 68
Musée d'Ethnographie du Trocadéro 27
myths 39, 45, 48

narratives 2, 24, 56, 59, 65, 89–91, 93; colonial 18, 30; cultural 92; elimination 67, 74; fetishistic slave 17; fictional 56; filmic 29–30, 49; pornographic films 30–1, 51; racialised 59
Nash, Jennifer 17, 26, 54, 76, 85–6
nation building 50, 85
nation states 58, 98
national masculinity 33
nationalism 7, 24, 33, 39, 44, 71, 98
Native 2, 16–17, 58–61, 63–5, 67–70, 74–5; Americans 16, 60, 63–7; audiences 76; culture 67; and Indigenous people 59–61, 67, 75; and interracial porn 59–60, 75; labour in colonies 15–16; lands 61; and non-Native sex 2; and pornography 2, 8, 17, 51, 59, 65, 67–8, 74–6, 94, 97; sex and nudity 28, 64, 67–8
natural rights 20, 79, 92–4
nature 6–7, 37–8, 48, 55, 65, 69, 92–4
neocolonial 19, 74, 79, 95, 98; cumshots 95; measures 48, 71; middle classes 93; representational strategies 35; structures 98; *see also* colonial
Non-Natives 60, 65, 67, 75
Northern Territory Government in Australia 6
Northern Territory National Emergency Response (referred to as The Intervention) 57, 71–3
nudity 28, 55–6

offences 72–3
orgasm 10, 20–2, 78, 80–1, 83–6, 88–91, 95–6, 99; cultural 85; earthshaking 22, 95; fake 22, 41, 82–3, 90, 95; female 22, 82, 90; *see also* male organism; *see also* female organism
orgies 47–8
Orientalist paintings 26–7, 38
Outback Assignment 25, 39, 41, 69, 71

paintings 26, 69, 92–3; of colonial labour 91; Modernist 28; Orientalist 26–7, 38; Picasso's Cubist 27
Papastephanou, Marianna 92
Patton, Cindy 80, 87
penetration scenes 75, 81
penial-vaginal intercourse 86
penises 80–2, 87, 96; disembodied 80
dismembered 87; ejaculating 80; imaged 87
perversion 1, 9–11, 57, 62, 83, 97
phallic pleasure 82
phantasma (of pornography) 7, 30
pharmacopornographic regimes 19, 79, 95, 97
photography 5–7, 11, 28
Pirates 29–30
pleasure 1, 20, 22, 26–7, 34, 47, 49, 53–4, 78, 81–3, 86, 88–91, 95, 97; experiencing 90; male 11, 78, 83; phallic 82; sexual 5
politics 12, 14–15, 24, 26, 53, 72–3; body 62; sexual identitarian 33, 51; shared 12
porn 1–13, 18–20, 22, 28, 30, 37–8, 54, 61, 63–5, 67–8, 71, 74–6, 78, 80, 85–9; actors 59–60, 68, 70, 90–1; anti-spectacular 10–11; contemporary 3, 71; feminists 11; food 10–11; industry 4, 65, 81; production 33, 68, 87; shoots 81; studies 2, 4, 7, 11, 15, 54, 86; videos 36
Porn Report in Australia 8
Pornhub 5, 63–5, 67–9, 73–5
pornoexotic 24–5, 28–32, 37, 39, 41, 50, 69–70; Australian 24, 31–7, 43–4, 49, 70; colonial 18, 31–2, 34, 48–9; films 34, 42

pornoexotica 28–9, 40, 44, 48, 54; colonial 18, 31–2, 34, 48–50; gay 33; straight 33
pornographic 4–5, 10, 12, 25, 27–31, 37, 55, 73, 75, 78; high budget films 32; imagery 5, 12, 98; images 5, 12; materials 72–3; photographs 5, 28, 31; photography 28; representations 13, 39, 54, 72, 78; stereotypes 67
pornography 1–13, 16–19, 22, 24–30, 32, 35, 48–9, 51, 53–76, 78, 81–9, 94–5, 98; banning of 18, 71–4; context of 4, 83; danger of 5, 18, 26–7; distribution of 9, 11, 73; racist 54; settler 24
pornstars 18, 35, 66–7, 71, 88
Povinelli, Elizabeth 55–7, 62, 99
Preciado, Paul B. 7, 19, 72, 97
properties 4, 8, 20–1, 48, 71, 74, 79, 83, 88, 92–5, 97–9; claims by settlers 18, 21, 48, 93–5; and natural rights 93

queer sex 9–10
queering (of Indigenous people) 61–2

Racial Discrimination Act 1975 6, 18, 71
racialisation 59–60, 68, 96–7
Radcliffe-Brown, Alfred 55
Rancière, Jacques 8–9, 12, 34, 63, 75
regimes 8–9, 34, 75, 95–6, 98; ideological 79; pharmacopornographic 19, 79, 95, 97; representational 97; somatic 19
reports 12, 72–3; *Little Children are Sacred* 6, 72; *Porn Report in Australia* 8
representational systems 1–2, 25
rewards 37, 49, 90–1
Reynold, Henry 92
rituals 48, 53, 56–7
Russell, Susie 71–2

Said, Edward 25
Second World War 14

semen 21, 80
settlements 2, 15–16, 46–9, 60–2, 79, 84, 92
settler colonies 7–8, 13–16, 18, 20–1, 24–5, 41, 43–4, 46–9, 54, 56, 59–60, 62, 84–5, 88–9, 91–2; comprising more men than women 46; European 50; ongoing 14–15; porn studies in 54
settler sexuality 2–3, 16–17, 20–2, 39, 41, 43, 48, 61, 67–8, 73–4, 78, 83–7, 89–90, 95, 98; centre of 73, 78; and modern sexuality 61; naturalising 2, 25, 50, 63; products of 7, 85; and settler immorality 62
settlers 2, 4, 17, 20–1, 31, 37–8, 53, 56, 58, 61–2, 67–8, 70–1, 76, 84–6, 91–4; colonialism 15, 31, 60; colonisation 13, 15, 19, 22, 56, 73–4, 83, 92; contemporary 94–5, 98; culture 67; heterosex 87; labour 20–1, 83, 90, 93; male white 18, 20, 68, 90, 93; non-Native 70; progressive 57; and properties 21, 93–4; structures 14, 85, 88
sex 1–4, 7, 9, 11, 16, 19–21, 27, 29–30, 33, 43–6, 48–51, 53, 55, 57–9, 84–7; colonial 40, 65; decolonising 98
sex scenes 37–8, 40–1, 49–51, 69–70, 81; 'failures' 38–9, 83, 88–9, 97; group 49; intercutting 49; male/female 37; outdoor 50
sex work 89–90
sex workers 8, 26, 28–9, 82
sexual abuse 72–4; *see also* sexual violence
sexual education 96
sexual fantasies 56
sexual medicine (nineteenth century) 96
sexual pleasure 5
sexual violence 2, 16, 20, 47–8, 59, 62, 72
sexuality 2, 8, 19–20, 49, 58, 61–2, 70, 72, 87; Aboriginal 72; modern 62, 65; natural 84, 94; 'primitive' 61; public 72; settler 2–3, 16–17,

sexuality continued
20–2, 39, 41, 43, 48, 61, 67–8, 73–4, 78, 83–7, 89–90, 95, 98; unrestrained 26; white 27
slavery 59
Smith, Paul 22, 63, 83
Smyth, Arthur 47–8
Snow, Donald 42
social media 12–13
Solomon-Godeau, Abigail 5, 34
Spencer, Baldwin 55
stag films 80–1
Stardust, Zahra 30, 32
stereotypes 28–9, 34–6, 54, 59, 61; activating 25; dangerous 87; identifiable 75; pornographic 67; reinstated 72; sexualised 28
Stoler, Laura 61–2, 96

terms 3, 9, 11, 13–14, 16–17, 19, 31, 63, 68, 91; colonial 63; cruel 35; porn/heteroporn 3; racialised 63
Theroux, Paul 31
Top 20: Native American Pornstars 66
Tourism Australia 34–6, 93
Tuck, Greg 16, 18, 20–1, 58, 60, 67, 82, 94, 97

United Nations General Assembly 58

vaginal intercourse *see also* intercourse 89
Veracini, Lorenzo 13–16

Victoria Blue 25, 40–1
videos 6, 12, 64–5, 67, 69, 74–5; amateur 67; professional Native 65
viewers 1, 3, 6, 9, 25, 27–9, 69, 78, 80, 85–7, 90, 95; and cumshots 85, 87; male 19, 81, 87–8
viewership 21, 31, 63
visual codes 7, 82

Warner, Michael 49, 84
White, Ricky 65
white Australian audiences 32
white women 27, 36, 48, 59
wild animals 34, 39
Williams, Linda 1, 4, 78, 80, 82–3
Wolfe, Patrick 7, 16, 21, 24, 56, 59–60
women 6, 12, 26–7, 36, 44, 46–9, 59, 66, 72–3; Black 55; colonisers 46; non-Native 74–5; and their exposed bodies 49; white 27, 36, 48, 59
Woodman, Pierre 25
work 7, 20–2, 26–7, 37, 43, 45–6, 50, 55, 82–3, 89–91, 93, 95, 97–8; of colonisation 45, 62, 91; emotional 89; institutionalised 91; sex 89–90

Yang, Wayne K. 16, 18, 20–1, 58, 60, 67, 94
YouPorn 63–4, 68–9

Žižek, Slavoj 29–30

Printed in the United States
by Baker & Taylor Publisher Services